DEPLOYABLE STRUCTURES

Published in 2015 by
Laurence King Publishing Ltd
361–373 City Road
London EC1V 1LR
United Kingdom
email: enquiries@laurenceking.com
www.laurenceking.com

A catalogue record for this book is available
from the British Library

ISBN: 978 1 78067 483 4

Design by & SMITH
Cover designed by Pentagram

Printed in China

Esther Rivas Adrover has experience as an architectural
practitioner and educator. After teaching Advanced
Descriptive Geometry to architecture students in Spain
she studied architecture at Oxford Brookes University
where she later taught at degree and postgraduate level.
Her interest in complex geometries led her to work for
practices including Zaha Hadid Architects, where she
worked on various projects in the UK and around the
world. She has also exhibited her own work several times
at the Royal Academy of Arts.

Deployable Structures

ESTHER RIVAS ADROVER

LAURENCE KING PUBLISHING

CONTENTS

1.0

2.0

FOREWORDS

In *The Seven Lamps of Architecture*, written in 1849 at the height of the Industrial Revolution, John Ruskin drew a boundary around the definition of architecture that rejected the then-emerging steel structures as a corrosive influence on the pure principles of timeless static stone.

Le Corbusier exploded this definition in the early twentieth century, declaring the house to be a 'machine for living' and setting the scene for a new architecture that would embrace the emerging technologies.

In the 1960s Ron Herron of Archigram proposed the 'Walking City' and in the BBC's 1989 television series *Building Sites* Norman Foster chose the jumbo jet as his favourite building.

With this trajectory, a book reviewing the influence of deployable structures on architecture seems like a natural progression. Esther Rivas Adrover's opening sentence – 'This book is living proof of the intrinsic synergy that connects all life with architecture' – proposes an exciting new chapter in the history of the 'Mother of the Arts'.

Within this emerging field the author proposes a classification of deployable structures, providing an interesting basis for a structured approach to thinking about the typologies that have been developed and illustrating clearly the potential of a dynamic architecture.

Architects will find in this book many inspiring examples of ingenious ways of transforming structures to create a responsive, organic architecture. Structural engineers will be stimulated to equip themselves with a deeper understanding of how they can support the flights of fancy that will inevitably emerge from the architect's imagination, as they extend their palette to incorporate this challenging new technology.

TIM MACFARLANE, 08 NOVEMBER 2014.
Founder of Dewhurst Macfarlane and Partners in 1985
Founder of Glass Light and Special Structures in 2012

Open Esther Rivas Adrover's book and you have deployed it. It's the start of a fascinating trail from folding (*ori-*) paper (*-kami*) to unfolding buildings. The magic of nature's *ori* never fails me. The unfolding poppy petal conceals so much. Where do the creases go? The wings of a newly emerged butterfly will expand even when cut away from the insect's body. What tricks is nature showing us that we have yet to see?

Deployment is a basic attribute of living organisms, whether as growth (deployment of cells) or movement (stretch out your arm – you are deploying it!). Perhaps this is why deployment is such a fascinating topic: inert mechanisms and objects become live and moving. The bird, and the beetle alike, can protect its wings by folding them away and, in its new streamlined form, invade new areas; while the dragonfly, which can't fold its wings, has to fly and roost in open spaces. A moth can have red or yellow hindwings, folded beneath the forewings; when disturbed it deploys its camouflaging forewings and flashes bright warnings. And it feeds through a tube that it keeps coiled away beneath its head. Cunning systems of levers and joints open and close roofs and the mouths of fish. The elastic-powered pipe-fish can suck in its prey in milliseconds: now you see it … now you don't!

Maxwell's Lemma tells us that the lightest (and therefore cheapest) structure separates compressive and tensile elements: the prescription for tensegrity. So we find such structures in outer and in inner space – satellite masts and cells use the same principles to keep and extend their shape. Can we learn from Maxwell how to deploy our resources to greater effect? Is this Esther Rivas Adrover's most important message?

JULIAN VINCENT, 10 NOVEMBER 2014.
Professor of Biomimetics at the University of Bath

PREFACE

This book is living proof of the intrinsic synergy that connects all life with architecture. I have always believed that everything is connected: give me any two apparently disparate elements, and I will find a connection between them – and architecture. 'Syntegration' is a term that I propose as a portmanteau of 'synergetic' and 'integration', and it is explained in the final chapter of this book.

But what does a carnivorous plant have to do with architecture? The research conducted on this emerging field has taken various interesting turns, and a curious example is a fascinating study of the carnivorous plant *Aldrovanda vesiculosa* (see p139). However, despite my 'syntegric' approach, I never expected to become a member of the International Carnivorous Plant Society as part of this journey!

From my chair I have travelled to the International Space Station, where ingenious masts have been used to deploy solar arrays effortlessly. Solar-powered satellite systems can be up to 1 kilometre (0.6 miles) long, vast structures the size of London's Regent's Park orbiting in silence, in space.

From intricate structures floating in space to organisms 5 millimetres (0.2 inches) small living under water, one could say that *Deployable Structures* can take you to any part of the Earth and beyond, quite literally. It would seem as if deployable structures can acquire meaning almost universally. But how can we travel around such vast and open coordinates with a sense of direction? Can any map connect such apparently disparate subjects? And how does that reconcile with architecture? The key is in 'Geometric Syntegration'.

No one knows everything about anything, thus there is a great deal yet to be learned, and never more so than about the incongruous subject of Deployable Structures in Architecture.

Fig 1. Space Elevator, by Esther Rivas Adrover

INTRODUCTION

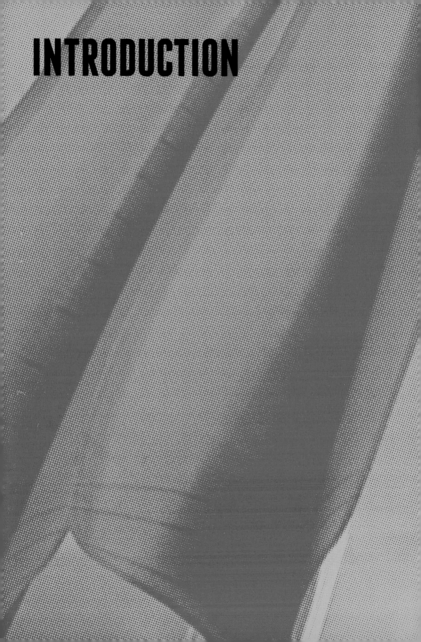

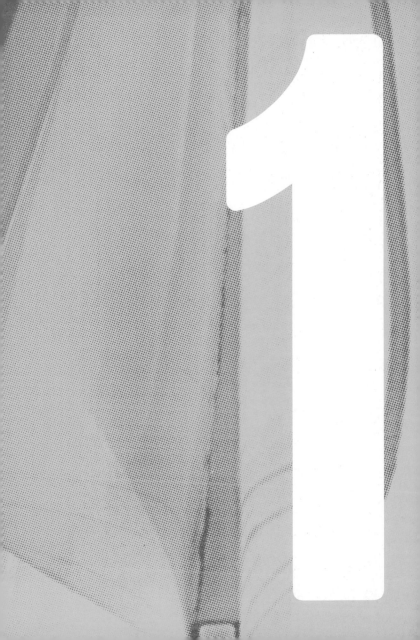

INTRODUCTION

Kinetic design and deployable structures have been used throughout history, but it was not until the beginning of the twentieth century that there was an emergence of thought inspired by the speed and technological advances of the Industrial Revolution. Movements such as Italian Futurism and schools such as the Bauhaus in Germany formed a cradle of ideas including kinetic principles that were explored in art, industrial design and architecture. These early explorations looked to challenge the establishment and its static convention, introducing the fourth dimension of Time as a key element of the process of transformation (RA 2014).

In the 1950s the aerospace industry took an interest in deployable structures, and today probably dominates the research in this field. Deployable structures have found many uses in this industry. Large structures such as satellites, telescopes, solar arrays and antennas have to be packaged in much smaller volumes in spacecraft, and once in space they are deployed.

Transportation has also been a concern for earth-bound applications. Today there is also strong research being carried out on mobile and rapidly assembled structures, mostly made of lightweight deployable structures, for adaptable building layers and for mobile or temporary applications, such as emergency shelters for disaster relief or military operations.

As this is still an emerging field, there is no single agreed definition of a deployable structure. These structures are sometimes referred to as foldable, reconfigurable, unfurlable, auxetic, extendible or expandable structures; however, they are perhaps best understood from these descriptions:

Deployable structures are structures capable of large configuration changes in an autonomous way.

TIBERT, 2002, P1

Such structures may pass from a 'folded' to an 'erect' state; and in many cases the component parts are connected throughout topologically, but alter their geometry through the process of deployment. In the process of deployment the initial mobility is transformed into a final rigidity. But that is by no means the only possible scheme for structural deployment.

CALLADINE, 2001, P64

By the application of a force at one or more points, it [a deployable structure] *transforms in a fluid and controlled manner. Despite such ease of transformation, these structures are stable, strong and durable.*

HOBERMAN, 2004, P72

The following is the author's own definition, which, it is believed, can be applied to any deployable type:

Deployable structures can expand and/or contract due to their geometrical, material and mechanical properties.

It would seem that deployable structures offer great potential for creating truly transforming, dynamic experiences and environments. Their lightness and transportability allow them to adapt to a society that is constantly evolving and changing. Furthermore, these are reusable structures that make efficient use of energy, resources, materials and space, thus embracing the concept of sustainability.

Today, not only engineers and architects, but origami scientists, biomimetic researchers, astrophysicists, mathematicians, biologists, artists and others are studying, designing and developing applications for an extraordinarily vast range of deployable structures. This includes mechanisms that have yet to be tested in architectural applications and are relatively unknown outside their scientific field. From these, the author has selected a variety of deployable structures (or principles) believed to have potential for technology transfer into architecture and design. This research also includes built projects and prototypes that are deployable or contain deployable elements.

This selection of deployables has been classified in typologies, classes and subclasses, shown in a tree diagram created and used as a navigational map, on pages 18–19.

This is novel design space.

DEPLOYABLE TYPOLOGIES

We are at an early, formative stage of its development, where we know and understand relatively little; where experiments are of the essence; where there are plenty of surprises in store; and where we have a long way before we reach that remote state where 'principles' can be enunciated and the whole business reduced to a branch of axiomatics.

CALLADINE, 2001, P64

This emerging field is rapidly changing and evolving in unpredictable ways. Research in this subject is carried out in disparate scientific fields, which do not necessarily always meet. But equally, many deployable inventions come from people who are not formally carrying out scientific research, such as artists. It is a field where applications spread across unforeseeable territories such as medicine, aerospace, art, industrial design, stage design, architecture, portable architecture, military equipment, infrastructure, vehicle components and fashion. Simultaneously, there are deployable structures for which no application has been found. Beyond pragmatic applications, deployable structures can also have philosophical implications (explored in Responsiveness, p146). The nature of this subject also seems to lie on the border of other research lines, such as robotics, biomimetics and material science. The scale of deployable mechanisms can range from a few millimetres (such as a deployable stent graft that can open a narrowed artery to treat oesophageal cancer; Kuribayashi, 2004) to vast structures that extend over thousands of metres (such as solar arrays deployed in space). Furthermore, this is a subject where ideas emerge that are difficult to articulate in words, and concepts can be best understood by acquiring experience with those deployable objects themselves, rather than entangling ideas in semantics and sophisms.

All these unattainably vast and incongruous parameters in which deployable structures operate seem to have made the task of giving an overall view of the subject a difficult one.

In 1973 Frei Otto classified typologies for deployable roof systems. Other classifications have been developed based on their one- or two-dimensional structural elements. There is also a classification by Ariel Hanaor for deployable structures capable of creating an enclosure, based on their morphology and their kinematic behaviour (De Temmerman et al, 2014).

The following is a holistic classification of a selection of deployables that offers an introduction to the subject and was carried out during my postgraduate studies in 2006 at the Oxford School of Architecture.

The principal issue that becomes apparent when attempting to classify deployable structures is that there are in fact two distinct approaches to developing a deployable. The first one is based on the structural components of the deployable mechanism: structures using this approach are classified under Structural Components. The second concentrates on movement and form inspired by various sources; these structures are described under the heading Generative Technique.

Two general types of Structural Components have been identified by experts in this field. These are Rigid

Component Deployables and Deformable Component Deployables (You, 2006). These two main types have been used as a starting point for creating an assembly of typologies (including classes and subclasses) with potential for architecture and design. Other structural typologies cannot be classified within these two main existing types, thus other main types are created, Flexible Deployables and Combined Deployables.

Generative Technique includes deployable principles inspired by origami and paper pleat techniques, and systems inspired by biological phenomenology (a field known as biomimetics, i.e. morphology and motion in animals and plants). Generative Technique thus contains deployable studies which have originated through conceptual principles and can later be developed with numerous structural systems.

These deployables, which have until now remained as isolated pieces of research, have been placed in an architectural context by adding examples of built projects and prototypes that are deployable, or contain deployable elements, thus illustrating the potential of technology transfer of deployable concepts in architecture.

The tree diagram presented on the following page displays the selection and classification of over thirty deployables and it aims to highlight the diversity (not quantity) of deployable approaches and to introduce this emerging field to the reader.

It is impossible to approach the field of deployable structures with a single, general concept or theory.

MIURA AND PELLEGRINO, 1999

TREE DIAGRAM

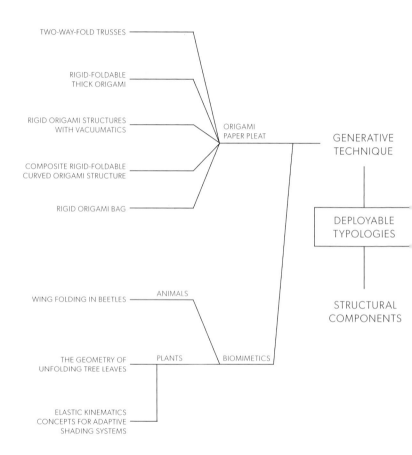

TWO-WAY-FOLD TRUSSES

RIGID-FOLDABLE
THICK ORIGAMI

RIGID ORIGAMI STRUCTURES
WITH VACUUMATICS

COMPOSITE RIGID-FOLDABLE
CURVED ORIGAMI STRUCTURE

RIGID ORIGAMI BAG

ORIGAMI
PAPER PLEAT

GENERATIVE
TECHNIQUE

DEPLOYABLE
TYPOLOGIES

STRUCTURAL
COMPONENTS

WING FOLDING IN BEETLES

ANIMALS

THE GEOMETRY OF
UNFOLDING TREE LEAVES

PLANTS

BIOMIMETICS

ELASTIC KINEMATICS
CONCEPTS FOR ADAPTIVE
SHADING SYSTEMS

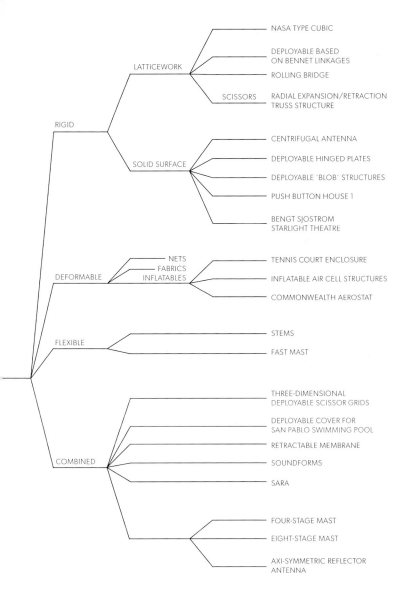

RIGID
  LATTICEWORK
    NASA TYPE CUBIC
    DEPLOYABLE BASED ON BENNET LINKAGES
    ROLLING BRIDGE
    SCISSORS
      RADIAL EXPANSION/RETRACTION TRUSS STRUCTURE
  SOLID SURFACE
    CENTRIFUGAL ANTENNA
    DEPLOYABLE HINGED PLATES
    DEPLOYABLE 'BLOB' STRUCTURES
    PUSH BUTTON HOUSE 1
    BENGT SJOSTROM STARLIGHT THEATRE

DEFORMABLE
  NETS
  FABRICS
  INFLATABLES
    TENNIS COURT ENCLOSURE
    INFLATABLE AIR CELL STRUCTURES
    COMMONWEALTH AEROSTAT

FLEXIBLE
  STEMS
  FAST MAST

COMBINED
  THREE-DIMENSIONAL DEPLOYABLE SCISSOR GRIDS
  DEPLOYABLE COVER FOR SAN PABLO SWIMMING POOL
  RETRACTABLE MEMBRANE
  SOUNDFORMS
  SARA
  FOUR-STAGE MAST
  EIGHT-STAGE MAST
  AXI-SYMMETRIC REFLECTOR ANTENNA

STRUCTURAL COMPONENTS

2.1 / STRUCTURAL COMPONENTS / RIGID

This type of deployable includes mechanisms made of rigid components. Their deployment process is fully controlled and the structure is stable at all stages of deployment.

Rigid-component deployables are considered to have great durability and have the most applications in architecture.

Deployables in this group are differentiated principally by the skin of their components. As a first general differentiation the skin can be made either of solid surfaces or latticework.

LATTICEWORK

These deployables have the minimum necessary structure to create the surface and the fold. The following latticework examples are differentiated by their mechanical geometry.

NASA Type Cubic
Alan L. Britt and Haresh Lalvani

This research project originates from the analysis of several deployable truss structures devised by Alan Britt for NASA (the National Aeronautics and Space Administration in the United States) in 1997 in the Morphology Studio of the Pratt Institute's School of Architecture, New York, and in the studies done by Haresh Lalvani in the mid 1970s of topology and symmetry transformation.

Fig 1. Deployment sequence of NASA's PACTRUSS geometry model.

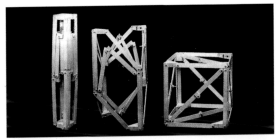

Fig 2. Deployment sequence of NASA's X-BEAM geometry model.

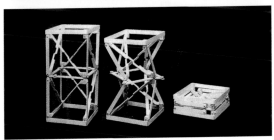

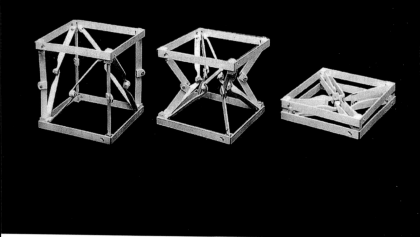

Fig 3. Deployment sequence of NASA's
STAC-BEAM geometry model.

The team aims to define a morphological design method that
can generate deployable structures based on crystallographic
symmetry and on variants of three NASA structures, the
PACTRUSS, the X-BEAM and the STAC-BEAM. The latter two are
used as extendable support structures for platforms such as solar
concentrators and phased arrays. In order to define their structural
morphology the team develops a four-letter notation (t, b, v, d) that
corresponds to the four structural component groups of a cubic
cell. The first letter (t) corresponds to the top horizontal members,
the second (b) to the bottom horizontal members, the third (v) to
the vertical members and the fourth (d) to the diagonal members.

The notation then describes whether the member is rigid (r) or
hinged (h). The morphological notation for the PACTRUSS
seen in figure 1 is (h, h, r, h) (representing hinged top members,
hinged bottom members, rigid vertical members and hinged
diagonal members).

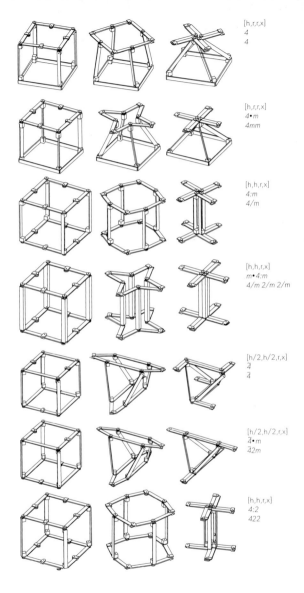

Figs 4–10. Deployment sequence of deployable structures representing each of the seven symmetry classes of order four.

[h,r,r,x]
4
4

[h,r,r,x]
4•m
4mm

[h,h,r,x]
4:m
4/m

[h,h,r,x]
m•4:m
4/m 2/m 2/m

[h/2,h/2,r,x]
4̄
4̄

[h/2,h/2,r,x]
4̄•m
4̄2m

[h,h,r,x]
4:2
422

Then the structural transformations based on the symmetry changes are defined, and range within orders four, two or one, based on the existing Shubnikov–Koptsik symmetry notation and Buerger's International notation. Figures 4 to 10 show deployable structures from order four. (Note that for the sake of clarity the diagrams do not include the diagonal members, and also that all the vertical members are rigid.)

These morphological tests are essential to detect design problems and to generate solutions to critical design issues such as strut and node morphology, and deployment path geometry.

Figure 11 shows an alternative design to the deployable structure seen in Figure 7 with a morphological notation (h, h, h, h) that allows greater compactness when the structure is in the packaged state.

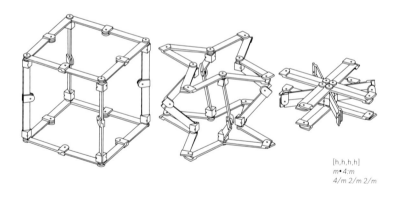

[h,h,h,h]
m•4:m
4/m 2/m 2/m

Fig 11. Variation of Figure 7 with identical symmetry but exhibiting a morphological change that allows greater compactness.

Deployable Structure Based on Bennett Linkages

Yan Chen and Zhong You

US Patent Number: 6,941,704 B2, 2005

Chen and You have developed a series of mechanisms that deploy smoothly into arches, towers and tent-like structures. These mechanisms are based on particular arrangements of 'Bennett linkages'. Presented here is one of those arrangements, which deploys into a tent-like shape and has been patented in the United States.

Figure 1 illustrates the deployment of a Bennett linkage. This mechanism was devised in 1903 by Geoffrey Thomas Bennett and consists of four rods connected in a loop with rotational joints that move in three dimensions.

Chen and You's invention consists of a geometrical array of interconnected rigid bars (Bennett linkages) connected by rotational joints, forming a structure that can expand in one direction only, and that deploys in a curved form.

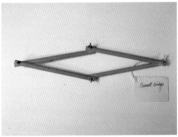

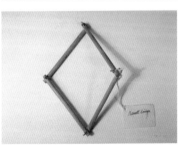
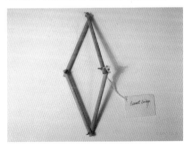

Fig 1. Deployment sequence of a Bennett linkage.

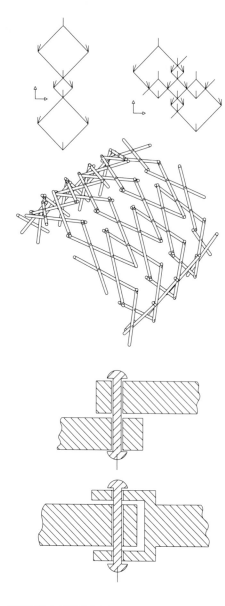

Fig 2. Top: schematic view of two Bennett linkages of the structural mechanism with a further alternative linkage. Below: perspective view of the structural mechanism in a curved state.

Fig 3. Cross section of alternative joints connecting two links.

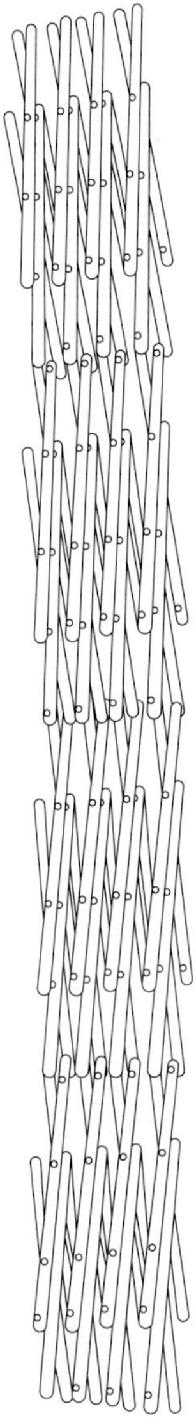

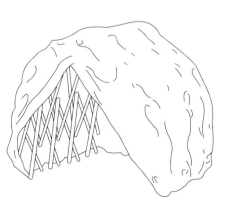

Fig 4. Perspective view of a structural mechanism in its flat state.

Fig 5. View of the structural mechanism used as a tent.

Rolling Bridge
Paddington Basin, London, United Kingdom, 2004
Heatherwick Studio

This deployable bridge consists of eight modules. Each module
is formed of two fixed trapezoidal steel frames on either side of a
section of deck at the base. The base of each module is hinged to
the next, with two pinned rigid struts linking each trapezoidal frame
at its top. Hydraulic rams linked to these pinned struts generate the
movement to deploy the structure. As the rams extend, the rigid
struts fold and the modules move, causing the bridge to curl back
on to itself, forming a circle on one side of the basin. When the
bridge is deployed, the tops of the frames and the struts between
them form the handrails, with the rams set into them.

Fig 1. Pinned struts forming the
handrails, with hydraulic ram actuator.

Fig 2. Deployment motion of the bridge.

SCISSORS

The folding chair made of two movable wooden frames connected to each other by pins was conceivably the first scissor structure ever devised. Although designs were patented in the nineteenth century, folding chairs were first used more than 4,000 years ago in ancient Egypt.

In the Italian Renaissance of the fifteenth and sixteenth centuries the polymath Leonardo da Vinci devised various sophisticated scissor structures that consisted of several modules of different sizes.

A considerable advance was made in the 1960s by the Spanish architect Emilio Pérez Piñero, who invented scissor-like structures that deployed in three dimensions. These principles were later developed further by Félix Escrig, Juan Pérez Valcárcel and José Sanchez.

A recent development in the design of scissor-like structures has been the invention of angulated scissors by Chuck Hoberman. A single angulated structure is made out of two symmetric bars hinged and kinked in the centre.

Today a great variety of scissor structures have been developed in a wide range of scales and forms. Their relatively simple construction system, using pivots, makes them very appealing. As well as being versatile, they are also very durable.

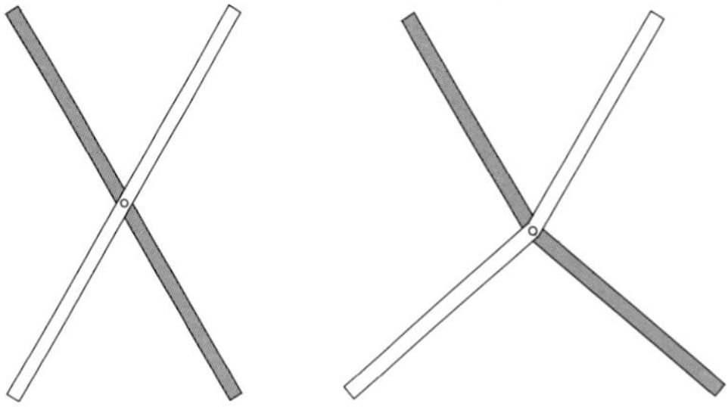

Fig 1. Left: straight scissors. Right: angulated scissors, invented by Chuck Hoberman.

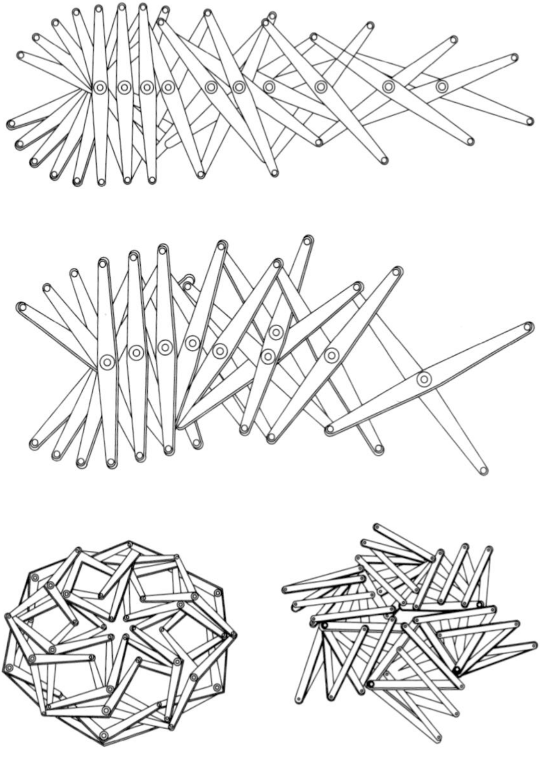

Fig 2. The deployable mechanisms of Hoberman scissors. From top to bottom: straight scissors with central pivot; straight scissors with offset pivot; angulated scissors (bottom left); swivel diagram (bottom right).

Radial Expansion/Retraction Truss Structures
Charles (Chuck) Hoberman
US Patent Number: 5,024,031, 1991

The key component of these kinetic structures is a single angulated scissor element designed by Hoberman (see p35).

The principle of the deployable structure is that it is made of at least three scissors-pairs with at least two of the pairs consisting of two equal rigid angulated bars. Each bar has three pivot points that are not co-linear, one central and one at each end, which form a deployable loop assembly. If a line were drawn intersecting the axes of the pivot points, it would not be parallel to at least two other such lines. The angles formed between those lines remain constant as the structure deploys.

These parameters can result in various arrangements. Figures 1, 2 and 3 show a range of structures; planar and three-dimensional, with iris and oval formations. These ideas have been used for architectural projects such as the Iris Dome for the World's Fair (Expo 2000) in Hanover, Germany; and the Olympic Arch for the 2002 Winter Olympics in Salt Lake City, Utah, USA.

Fig 1. Deployment sequence of a planar retractable structure in an iris-type formation.

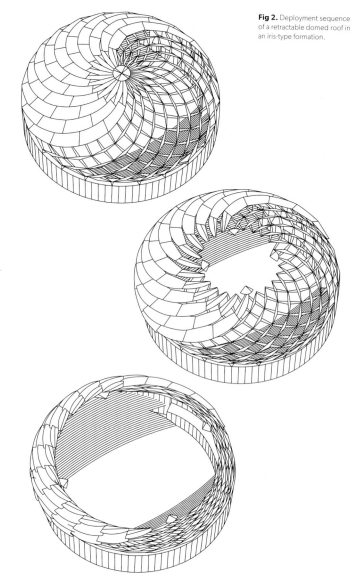

Fig 2. Deployment sequence of a retractable domed roof in an iris-type formation.

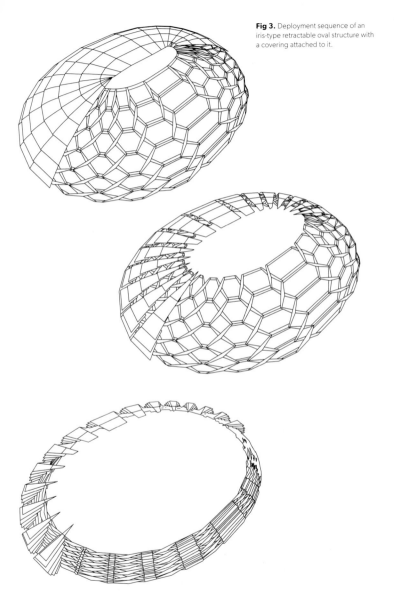

Fig 3. Deployment sequence of an iris-type retractable oval structure with a covering attached to it.

SOLID SURFACE

These deployable mechanisms consist of connected rigid panels, and they are a popular choice in the worlds of architecture and industrial design.

Solid vertical panels that slide on rails and create flexible spaces are a basic form of this mechanism, and have been used since ancient times in Japan, where they are known as *shoji* screens.

This concept has been used in projects such as Gerrit Rietveld's Rietveld Schröder House, in Utrecht, the Netherlands, built in 1924 and inspired by the work of artist Piet Mondrian.

The Maison de Verre (Glass House), built in Paris in 1932 and designed by the architect Bernard Bijvoet, the industrial designer Pierre Chareau and the craftsman-metalworker Louis Dalbet, is also an important example of architecture that uses deployable solid screens. In this project it is not just walls that slide: deployable industrial design emerges in the most unexpected places, such as the bathroom. A simple and elegant example is an articulated desk made out of metal 'petals' that open out from a single pivot.

The first large-scale built project in the world with deployable solid panels was the Civic Arena in Pittsburgh, Pennsylvania, by the architects Mitchell & Ritchey and the engineers Ammann & Whitney. (This project was built in 1961, and, notwithstanding its undeniable historic importance, it was demolished in 2012, despite strong opposition from preservation groups.)

It consisted of a dome made of eight 'petals', of which six were equipped with wheels that were set upon an annular track. The petals would fold back upon themselves, exposing the proscenium. Two of those petals were permanently static and attached to a substantial 79-metre-long (260 foot) cantilevered arm. The six kinetic petals could form a deployable structure of 12,500 square metres (14,350 square yards) and weighing 300 tonnes that could deploy in under three minutes, in a concentric motion powered by hydraulic jacks.

Although nowadays there are various large stadia with deployable roofs, the Civic Arena was unique, as the entire envelope of the building could be deployed (not just its roof). Thus, when opened, it created a completely open-air theatre. Its ingenious design placed the concrete ring girder, upon which the petals rested, totally separate from and offset to the stadium seat structure.

In 2003 the construction of the Qizhong International Tennis Centre, Shanghai, was completed. Designed by the architect Mitsuru Senda of EDI, the eight-segment retractable flat roof requires eight minutes to deploy, powered electrically. Each petal is pinned in one corner only. The geometry of the roof allows each petal to rotate around its single pin on an arc track on the adjacent module that guides movement.

The following examples are a series of built projects, prototypes and aerospace deployable mechanisms that consist of solid surfaces.

Centrifugal Antenna

Tomomi Kanemitsu, Shinji Matsumoto, Haruyuki Namba,
Takanori Sato, Hisato Tadokoro, Takao Oura, Kenji Takagi,
Shigeru Aoki and Nobuyuki Kaya

This team has designed an antenna that can self-deploy in space using its centrifugal force, a radial force that expands from the centre of a rotating body. Applications include Solar Power Satellite Systems (SPSS), which use solar battery panels with a diameter that can vary between 100 to 1,000 metres (110 to 1,093 yards).

When stowed, the antenna has a polygonal column configuration with a height of 1 metre (3.3 feet) and a diameter of 0.5 metres (1.6 feet). Once completely deployed, it transforms into a hexagonal polygonal disc 2 metres (6.6 feet) in diameter and 30 millimetres (1.2 inches) in thickness.

The antenna consists of six large trapezoidal parts assembled in a circumferential arrangement. Each of those trapezoidal parts is divided in a radial direction into 'n' segments. The segments are connected by universal hinges in the circumferential direction. In the radial direction the segments are connected by hinge joints (figure 1). The arrangement of these joints is dictated by the way in which the structure deploys geometrically and the thickness of the segments; in order to allow motion the hinge joints and the universal joints must be located on opposite surfaces. If one segment has two universal joints and one is located on the top surface, the other one must be located on the bottom surface, and likewise for hinge joints.

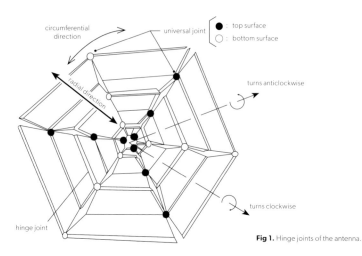

Fig 1. Hinge joints of the antenna.

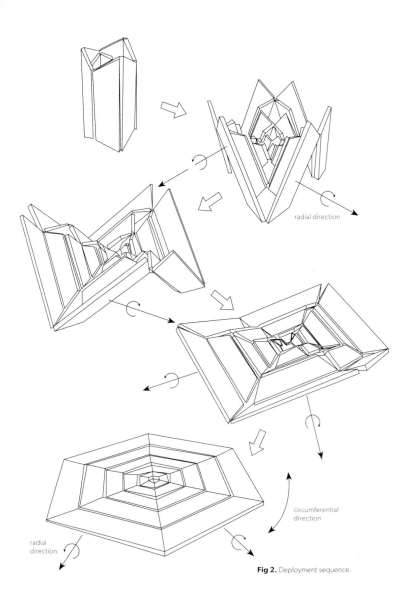

radial direction

circumferential direction

radial direction

Fig 2. Deployment sequence.

Deployable Hinged Plates

Frank Vadstrup Jensen and Sergio Pellegrino

This study proposes a new family of two-dimensional deployable structures made of flat plates connected by cylindrical scissor joints. This type of structure has no gaps when closed and forms a perfect circle when open, making it ideal for the design of retractable roofs.

The study is based on a novel concept of foldable bar structures made of 'multi-angulated' scissor hinges, developed by the engineering scientists Zhong You and Sergio Pellegrino. This principle can be applied in a variety of configurations (figures 1 and 2).

The study proposes replacing the bar structure with identical flat plates connected with cylindrical joints at precisely the same location as the original bar structure. Thus the end result is a double layer of flat plates with an identical kinematic behaviour to that of the scissor bar structure.

The original concept begins with identical flat plates defined by straight lines (figure 3). However, those straight lines cause the plates to jam in the initial motion of the structure's deployment. Therefore, a new boundary shape between the cover plates is being investigated (figures 4 and 5).

The resulting structure is a double layer of identical but inverted flat discs made of curved plates that open in a sequence reminiscent of that of a flower.

Figs 1–2. Deployment of bar structure with six cylindrical scissor joints.

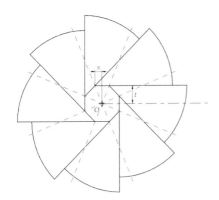

Fig 3. Opening sequence of cover plates with straight lines.

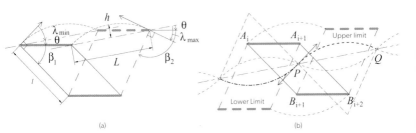

Fig 4. Geometric analysis that defines the region for possible boundary shapes.

(a)

(b)

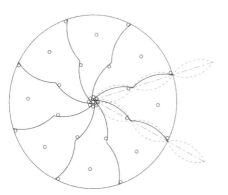

Fig 5. Curved region boundary shape in flat plates.

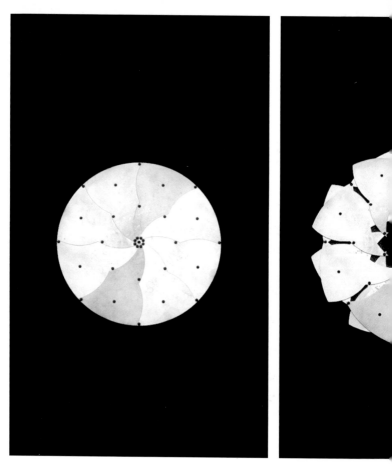

Figs 6–8. Deployment sequence
of a hinged plate structure with four
cylindrical scissor joints and eight
plates in each disc (or layer).

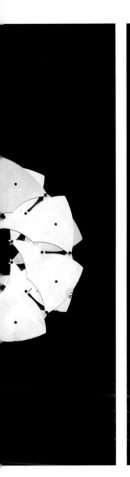

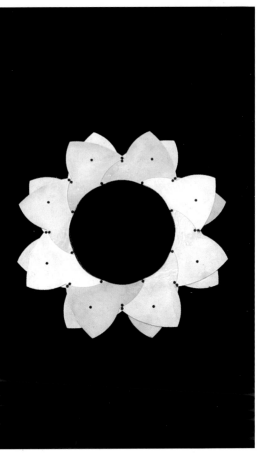

Deployable 'BLOB' Structures

Frank Vadstrup Jensen and Sergio Pellegrino

Vadstrup Jensen and Pellegrino have formulated a method for designing deployable free-form, three-dimensional structures with a single DOF (degree of freedom) by connecting two or more deployable hinged plates (see p44).

A key issue when defining the geometry of the plates was to determine the boundary shape. Vadstrup Jensen and Pellegrino have showed that this shape does not need to be identical for every plate. As long as the plate boundaries have a certain periodic geometry, the structure will deploy in harmony (figure 1).

In order to create a three-dimensional deployable structure, identical plates would be placed one on top of the other. That would mean, however, that the discs that face one another would rotate in opposite directions and connecting them would be difficult. But that problem can be solved by swapping the top and bottom layers of one of the plate structures. Doing this creates two structures with two facing discs with identical plates and motions, and thus the plates can be used to connect the two structures rigidly (figure 3).

Figures 4, 5 and 6 show the spherical solid rigid deployable structure resulting from the union of the identical facing plates. The plates are made of matching plastic structures that have been trimmed, to which blocks of light foam board have been glued, which were previously cut using abrasive water-jet cutting.

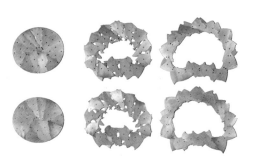

Fig 1. Deployment of non-circular model with all plate boundaries different, showing both layers.

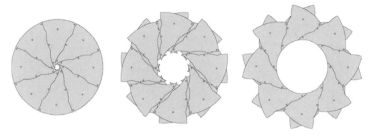

Fig 2. Deployable circular plate structure.

Fig 3. Perspective view of deployment
of spherical structure.

For two plates belonging to different deployable plate structures
to be connected rigidly and to be able to rotate in synchronized
motion, they must satisfy the single kinematic constraint of sharing
the same axes of rotation. As the kinematics of a plate structure are
equivalent to those of a bar structure, this study proposes that the
design of a deployable solid should be based on its underlying bar
structures and its axes of rotation.

Figure 7 shows two non-circular bar structures, one in a thinner line
(I) and the other in a thicker line (II). Kassabian, You and Pellegrino
(1999) have demonstrated that the axis of rotation of any angulated
element is at the halfway point between the origin of the polygon
(O) and the vertex defining the central hinge of the element.
Thus the hinges A belonging to bar structures I and II share the
axis of rotation A cen. A 'cen' is the resulting intersection of the
conceptual lines drawn from A II to O II and A I to O I. A cen
is also the centre point between A II to O II and A I to O I.

The same principles apply to B and C. Therefore the angulated elements of A, B, C of both structures can be rigidly connected by the triangles (shown in grey) that define the vertices of both structures and their common rotation axis.

In order to design a complex solid, its free-form geometry must first be defined (figure 8). The designer must then decide how many layers of blocks are going to be used and their underlying bars and plate structures, here shown in figure 6 as made of six identical angulated elements. Note that figure 9 displays the plates with circular arcs but their actual shape would be determined by the complex free-form solid. In order for this complex solid to deploy, the inner walls of the blocks need to be doubly curved.

Fig 7. Deployment of two stacked bar assemblies.

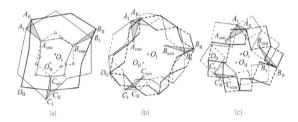

(a)　　　(b)　　　(c)

Fig 8. Perspective view of deployable 'BLOB' structure.

Fig 9. Plate structures for generation of solid blocks.

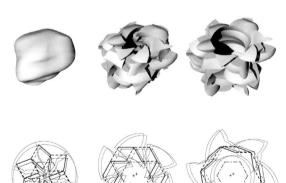

Push Button House 1
Adam Kalkin

This portable shipping container opens at the push of a button, revealing an apartment with six different living areas: a dining area, a kitchen, a double bedroom, a bathroom, a library and a living room.

The synchronized opening sequence utilizes eight hydraulic rams to move all the side planes of the shipping container in less than a minute, leaving as fixed elements only the top and bottom planes and the four corner posts. Both long sides of the container roll down, tripling the footprint of the main living area. The two ends deploy in two different ways: one opens as door pivots and the other extends floor and ceiling planes horizontally.

Figs 1–3. Opening sequence of the Push Button House 1.

Bengt Sjostrom Starlight Theatre

Rock Valley College, Rockville, Illinois, United States, 2003
Studio Gang Architects

Rock Valley College commissioned a theatre that could retain
the open-air feel of its existing auditorium, as well as guarantee
scheduled performances in summer despite changing weather
conditions. Studio Gang Architects proposed the idea of a
deployable roof, as well as designing facilities for an extended
theatre programme that were built in three phases.

In order to create a kinetic roof the architects collaborated with
engineers Uni-Systems. The faceted roof consists of triangular
stainless steel-clad panels sandwiched with glu-lam beams.
The plan of the roof when closed can be seen in figure 5.
The hexagonal array of triangulated panels at the centre forms
the kinetic part of the roof, which is supported by the permanent
structure's steel members. The central formation opens in a
clockwise motion in just over 10 minutes, and the cantilevered
triangulated panels, which each weigh 15 tonnes, lift silently. Each
moving triangulated panel has a gutter on the side, so that when
the roof is closed the guttering system extends all the way round
because of the clockwise interlocking system. Each panel has an
electronic gearbox and a back-up manual hydraulic operation system.

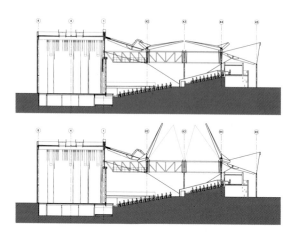

Fig 1. Building sections
showing the roof closed
(top) and open (bottom).

Fig 2. Roof open
(opposite).

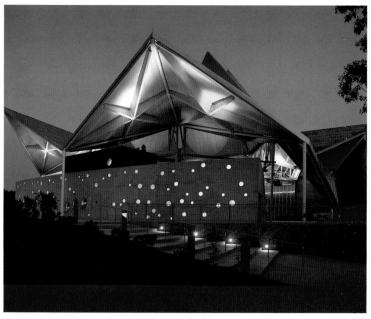

Fig 3. Night-time view (above).

Fig 4. View of the night sky through opened roof (left).

Fig 5. Roof plan (closed configuration, opposite).

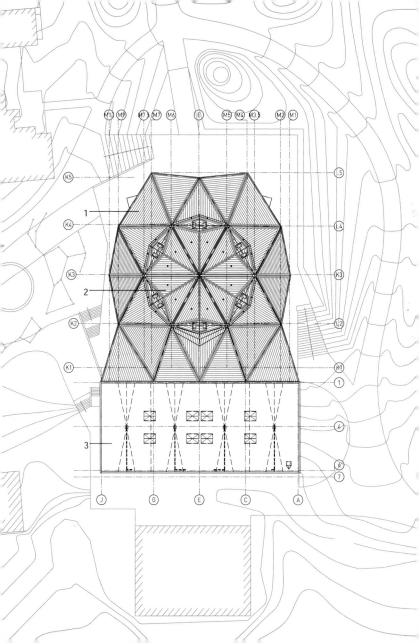

2.2 / STRUCTURAL COMPONENTS / DEFORMABLE

All the typologies of deployable structures, even those made with rigid components, deform slightly in the process of deployment, but this is negligible when compared to the huge changes that Deformable Deployables undergo. The basic types of Deformable Deployables are nets, fabrics and inflatables. Nets and fabrics are perhaps the oldest types and have found many uses through the centuries. Their deployment can only be controlled when they are combined with other structural components (see Combined Deployables, p74).

Inflatables, also named pneumatic structures, are not only versatile but can also be highly durable. Their extremely fast erection times and lightness have inspired interest in many disciplines.

The concept of inflatables probably began with the first hot-air balloons in the eighteenth century, with experiments such as the ones conducted by Bartolomeu de Gusmão (Chi and Pauletti, 2005) and later perfected by the Montgolfier brothers (Herzog and Minke, 1977). At the turn of the twentieth century inflatable principles were used for applications such as Zeppelins and temporary tents. The development of the latter was made possible after the invention of nylon, and they were used in World War II as emergency shelters and decoys.

Research in academia began in the 1960s with Frei Otto's form-finding investigations and designs. At the very same time and as part of independent research, the Italian architect Dante Bini pioneered the application of pneumatic formwork that allowed the erection of large concrete dome structures in just a few hours (Bini, 2014).

The apogee of pneumatic structures at that time has since inspired a great variety of ideas and projects, such as Richard Buckminster Fuller's utopian proposal of a pneumatic dome for New York City (Herzog and Minke, 1977), and the numerous Osaka Expo pneumatic pavilions in the 1970s.

Today, inflatable structures have found an immense variety of applications and they range from entertainment uses and applications in space to contemporary art projects, to mention but a few.

INFLATABLES

The manipulation of air in order to create structures and experiences can be done through numerous techniques. The following is a selection of built projects that illustrate the potential and the variety of inflatable principles at an architectural scale.

Tennis Court Enclosure

Coolhurst Tennis Club, London, UK, 2007
Paul Romain of Ingenu Engineers;
Birds Portchmouth Russum Architects

This versatile tennis enclosure is a 'super-pressure structure' made for Coolhurst Tennis Club and provides a safe environment in which to play tennis during the winter months. A super-pressure structure is made of a single skin of fabric that maintains its shape by having air pumped into it. The structure is completely sealed at the base, and entry and exit to the enclosure are through an airlock.

The structural envelope has a perimeter skirt made of robust white PVC and a translucent mesh reinforced PVC top that allows in light; either natural daylight or artificial light from the tennis floodlights at night. After being inflated, super-pressure structures require a constant flow of air in order to maintain the shape of the envelope in its deployed state. The air intake duct creates a permanent background noise. Although this sound is negligible for many users, it is important to note that it might not be appropriate for certain programmes or clients that require special acoustics or just simply silence.

As in the case of any inflatable enclosure, the anchoring of the envelope to the ground is a critical part of the structural strategy of the project.

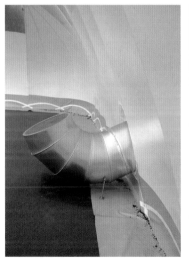

Figs 1–4. Interior view (opposite), exterior view (top), air intake duct (above left), set out of cover fully anchored to the ground ready for inflation (above right).

Inflatable Air Cell Structures
Magna Science Adventure Centre, Rotherham, UK, 2001
Lindstrand Technologies; Wilkinson Eyre Architects

The manipulation of fabric shaped by air can be used to achieve a vast range of structures. From inflatable dwellings held by super pressure or air cells, to airships, aerostats and gas balloons, Lindstrand Technologies operates in the fields of architecture and entertainment, and military and scientific research. Its innovation centre has designed inflatable tunnel plugs to extinguish fires and inflatable flood barriers, and has also built a parachute that was commissioned by the European Space Agency for a spacecraft dedicated to finding life on Mars.

The inflatable structures fabricated for the Magna Science Adventure Centre are collectively one of the most innovative ventures undertaken by Lindstrand Technologies. This educational visitor centre, designed by Wilkinson Eyre Architects and awarded the RIBA Stirling Prize in 2001, submerges the visitors in its interactive learning experiences through its five main pavilions: Earth, Air, Fire, Water and Power.

There are three main inflatable structures, interconnected with air-inflated fabric tunnels, which are fabricated with air-cell technology. The key aspect that defines the advanced structural capabilities of air cell technology is the array of fabric formers perpendicular to the two main external layers of material. These structures are self-supportable and self-erectable by the use of an air fan. They have great thermal and sound insulation properties as well as a high torsional stiffness, and if erected outdoors can have a lifespan of 10 or 20 years, depending on climatic conditions. Made entirely of fabric they can be easily packaged, transported and deployed in the desired location within a day.

Air cell structures are made of membrane fabrics composed of polyvinyl chloride (PVC) combined with other elements to achieve certain properties, such as flexibility. These polyester fabrics are cut according to CAD profiles by automated cutting machines. While the overall envelope is seamwelded, the three-dimensional framework is created by dropstitched panels. In certain areas the fabric panels will be reinforced in order to achieve the desired structural capability, and they will also have to be anchored appropriately on site. These structures also require connections for air inflation and extraction. While the air fan will operate on full power during the initial deployment of the structure, it will thereafter only respond to a drop in pressure.

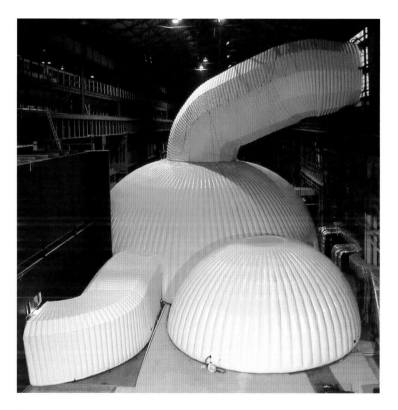

Fig 1. Magna's interconnected inflated air cell structures.

Commonwealth Aerostat

Delhi, India, 2010
Mark Fisher, Architect; Lindstrand Technologies;
Elementenergy

The 2010 Commonwealth Games in Delhi saw the rise of a large body emerging effortlessly into the air. This helium-filled aerostat, designed by the architect Mark Fisher, was the centrepiece for the opening ceremony of the Games. An aerostat gains its lift through its 'aerostatic' buoyant force by using a lighter-than-air gas, in this case helium. This aerostat was the largest in the world and was used as a 'white canvas' on which to project videos and images that would set the mood and rhythm of the ceremony. Its design is based on the geometry of a torus – a surface revolution generated by a circle revolving around a coplanar axis in three-dimensional space.

As with all their airships and inflatable structures, every single component of the aerostat was designed and manufactured in the Lindstrand factory. The aerostat's main structural component is its envelope, which is made with new composite aerostat skin materials with exceptionally low helium permeation. Six kilometres (3.7 miles) of fabric were used to make the structure, which was 80 metres (262 feet) long, 40 metres (131 feet) wide and 12 metres (39 feet) high. It was designed and built in four sections by using advanced fabric welding methods. These sections were designed to be joined using Dutch lacing and zips. The pressure of the aerostat was maintained by helium valves, ballonet fans and pressure-relief valves in each of the torus sections.

This gigantic aerostat was tethered to the ground with ropes connected to 10 specific structural points (emphasized by the airship 'skirt' with its oriental motifs).

Elementenergy was approached to provide assessment on the aerodynamic loads in order to ensure a safe deployment of the aerostat. Simulations were done in which the relation of weight and size was tested against wind conditions.

Fig 1. Daytime view of torus on site.

Fig 2. Night-time view of the opening ceremony.

2.3 / STRUCTURAL COMPONENTS / FLEXIBLE

This group describes deployables that cannot be classified within the previously identified Rigid or Deformable typologies. While rigid deployables go through negligible deformation during deployment, in contrast to deformable types, structures in this new group undergo some deformation in a fluid and controlled manner. This is because the components are semi-rigid and may flex in defined directions.

STEMs (Storable Tubular Extendible Member)
George J. Klein (STEM)
Astro Aerospace Corporation (Bi-STEM)
Andrew Daton-Lovett, Rola Tubes Ltd and DSL Cambridge (BRC: Bi-stable Reeled Composite)

The principle of a STEM, or tubular boom, is similar to that of the curved metal tape found in tape measures (figure 1).

STEMs are given a curved form by forcing a flat tape into a tubular mould and heating it so that the curved shape remains. Thus, when STEMs are extended they are not subject to stresses. In contrast, when they are coiled on to a drum they contain stored elastic energy, and it is this energy that powers their deployment. Among materials suitable for STEMs are fibreglass, beryllium-copper, Mylar, titanium and spring steel.

Figure 2 shows a Bi-STEM, which is made of two identical bands positioned one inside the other. A Bi-STEM will need smaller stowage drums and its deployment will be more stable than that of a STEM.

Interlocking Bi-STEMs (figure 3) provide the tubular boom with a higher torsional stiffness.

An extension of the STEM is the BRC (Bi-stable Reeled Composite), also known as the Bi-stable Laminated Composite Tube (figures 4 and 5). Although in appearance it is identical to a STEM, a BRC is stable in both deployed and stowed configurations. This is achieved by a particular layout of the fibres in the composite material. Today, Rola Tubes Ltd employs this technology in a vast number of applications, ranging from defence, space (including deployable tubular booms in space vehicles that extend cameras to film other planets), oil and gas, mining and civil engineering, and consumer products.

Fig 1. STEM.

Fig 2. Bi-STEM.

Fig 3. Interlocking Bi-STEM.

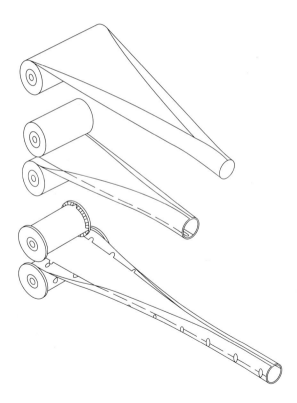

Fig 4. BRC rolled configuration.

Fig 5. BRC deployed configuration.

FAST Mast (Folding Articulated Square Truss Mast)

ATK Engineering Company, Space Components Division, California

This mast consists of revolute hinges along long cables forming square bays, with the hinge axes parallel to the sides of the bays, and two pairs of diagonal bracing cables on each face of the bays. The cables are stressed by four lateral bows. When the structure is folded, the bows bend and half of the bracing cables become slack, but they become fully stable when the mast is deployed. The mast is packaged within a canister, and its deployment is actuated by the strain energy stored in the four fibreglass bows of each bay. This principle is shown in figure 1.

This mast was used by NASA in the International Space Station to deploy solar arrays, which convert sunlight into electricity. Materials for coilable masts are currently carbon fibres, where previously fibreglass and then graphite fibres were used.

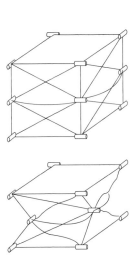

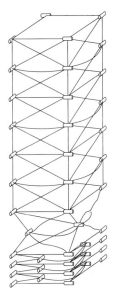

Fig 1. Principle of the FAST Mast.

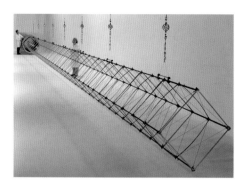

Fig 2. FAST Mast being tested.

Fig 3. NASA astronaut Clayton Anderson works during the third spacewalk of Space Shuttle mission STS-131 in 2010, with Earth and one of the International Space Station's solar arrays deployed by the FAST Mast as a backdrop.

Fig 4. Astronaut Steve Bowen works on one of the solar arrays and FAST Mast rotation joints during the first spacewalk of Space Shuttle mission STS-126 in 2008.

2.4 / STRUCTURAL COMPONENTS / COMBINED

This group includes deployables that combine different structural components, and that can contain rigid, deformable and/or flexible parts to create one mechanism.

In 1954 one of the American architect Richard Buckminster Fuller's geodesic domes was built by architecture students at Washington University, St. Louis, Missouri. Although other such structures had been built before this date, this was a *deployable* geodesic dome, and it consisted of solid rods tensioned by cables actuated by pneumatic cylinders. Today, the outdoor products company North Face produces a range of shelters based on Buckminster Fuller's geodesic principles, but made with very light materials that allow easy transportation and deployment.

In 1971 the German architects and engineers Frei Otto and Bodo Rasch designed an array of large deployable inverted umbrellas, each with a diameter of 19 metres (62 feet), for the Cologne Federal Garden Exhibition. This was a novel interpretation of the concept of the parasol, which has been used since the ancient world.

In the 1980s Dante Bini designed a building system (named Binistar) for a deployable structure that combines rigid members, connected to fabric, that lock into position through the process of pneumatic inflation. This system can be used to deploy a wide range of envelopes such as square-plan domes, and hexagonal and vaulted structures: an example of the last was the press centre for the 1990 FIFA football World Cup finals in Italy.

The contemporary range of applications of Combined Deployables is vast. The following deployable built projects and prototypes combine a variety of structural components.

Three-Dimensional Deployable Scissor Grids
Emilio Pérez Piñero, 1960s
Patent 3,185,164: Three-dimensional Reticular Structure, 25 May 1965

In 1961 an international competition for students of architecture in 54 countries was set up by the International Union of Architects and held in London. The theme was 'Transportable Theatre'. The renowned architects and engineers Buckminster Fuller, Félix Candela and Ove Arup were members of the jury. Emilio Pérez Piñero's proposal for a deployable structure won a special mention (figures 1 and 2).

Pérez Piñero further developed this principle, and in 1966 his concept for a 'Transportable Theatre' was made a reality and inaugurated in Plaza de María Pita de A Coruña, Spain (figure 3). The mobile deployable structure consisted of scissors of four arms made with aluminium bars, and could cover 8,000 square metres (9,567 square yards) and weigh 40 tonnes.

Pérez Piñero also experimented with various other models including one with scissors of three arms, which in 1965 was developed into a patent design consisting of three-arm scissor rods connected by pins mounted in coplanar positions (figure 4).

Fig 1. Proposal for a deployable dome for a 'Transportable Theatre' (1961): packaged state ready for transportation.

Fig 2. Proposal for a deployable dome for a 'Transportable Theatre' (1961): deployed state.

Fig 3. Inauguration of the 'Transportable Theatre' in Plaza de María Pita de A Coruña (1966).

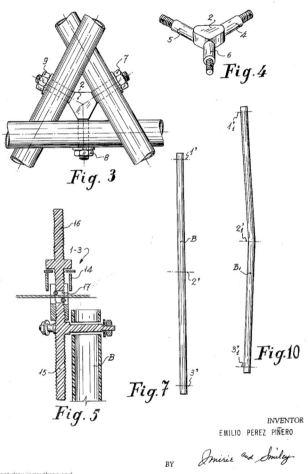

Fig. 3

Fig. 4

Fig. 5

Fig. 7

Fig. 10

INVENTOR

EMILIO PEREZ PIÑERO

BY   Imirie and Smiley

ATTORNEYS

Fig 4. Patent drawings: three-rod
connection to an intermediate coupling.

Deployable Cover for San Pablo Swimming Pool

Seville, Spain, 1996

Félix Escrig, Juan Pérez Valcárcel and José Sanchez

Escrig and his colleagues designed a cover, based on x-frame modules, for an Olympic-size swimming pool that could be suspended from a crane and deployed on site by gravity in only a matter of hours, and subsequently anchored into foundations and supports. During warm weather this cover could be removed, leaving the swimming pool completely open and without any visible trace of the cover's construction.

The structure is made of a scissor grid connected to a membrane. The team established a new system, based on the principle of simple scissors, that can be connected by hinges and that allows a much wider deployment than three- and four-arm scissor structures.

Figure 1 shows the design of the joints of the struts. Only four struts are connected at each joint and all bars have the same length (5.38 metres; 17.7 feet).

In order to prevent it becoming entangled during deployment, the fabric is hung on the lower level of the structure (figure 1), and connected to the diagonals of each quadrilateral module, as can be seen from the interior view shown in figure 8.

The stiffness of the scissor structure was analysed using special software in which a set of parameters could be inputted (such as span and weight of structural members). A 1:10 scale model was built in order to confirm the numerical results from the study and was tested with symmetrical and non-symmetrical loads (figure 2).

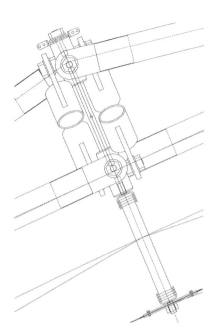

Fig 1. Connection of the fabric and the lower joints.

Fig 2. 1:10 scale model, non-symmetrically loaded.

Figs 3–8. Packaging, transportation and deployment sequence of the swimming pool cover on site.

Retractable Membrane

K. Kawaguchi

Kawaguchi proposes a new approach for retractable membrane roof-structure systems that consist of twisting a cylinder into a disc form.

Figure 1 shows two examples. Each end of the cylindrical membrane is connected to an end compression ring. The rings can be arranged so that both are at the top or one is placed at either end. They rotate in different directions, enabling the membrane to deploy.

For this principle to serve as a roof structure this membrane must be fully tensioned. Air pressure is one of the means explored. In the final configuration of deployment the surface consists of two membrane layers that can be inflated (figure 1). The structure thus becomes an inflatable roof – an air cell.

Another possibility would be to enclose the bottom of the cylinder and to introduce an air intake that would keep the roof membrane in tension (figure 2).

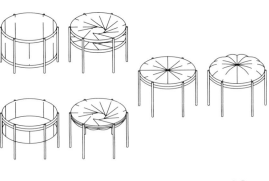

Fig 1. Retractable air-inflated membrane roof.

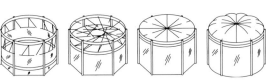

Fig 2. Retractable air-supported membrane roof.

Soundforms

2012

Mark Stephenson, Soundforms Ltd; Jason Flanagan
and Paul Bavister, Flanagan Lawrence; Ian Knowles,
Arup Acoustic; and ESGroup

Soundforms is the first outdoor portable stage that has been designed in order to achieve an ideal acoustic environment for the performers and the audience. Although this prototype is not, strictly speaking, a deployable structure, it incorporates some deployable principles and structural members that combine rigid and deformable components.

The team investigated three different types of acoustic performance: full symphony orchestra, string quartet and a small chamber ensemble. These conditions established a set of acoustic ratios that were distilled into a UK patent.

The projecting shell shape of the stage was the result of rigorous research into acoustic performance. The reflectors installed on to the fixed overhead of the stage deliver a dynamic on-stage acoustic reflection, allowing performers to hear one another and enhancing the sound ensemble and projection.

The structure is made of a series of interconnected arches that are assembled in a rotational motion and then fixed to the rotating pivot point. The covering skin is a PVC-coated polyester inflated surface formed by eight different panels that can be fixed with a series of airtight zips designed by NASA. The structure is anchored on the site by 40 tonnes of ballast, in the form of sand, water or concrete, which prevents it from lifting.

Fig 1. Close view of stage during
a performance.

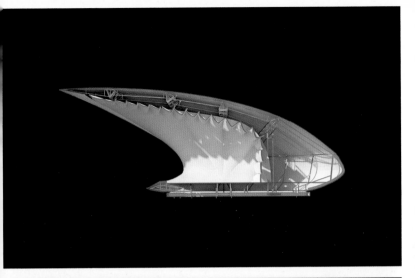

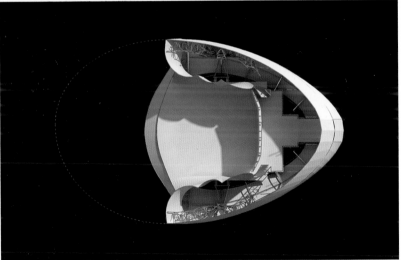

Figs 2–3. Cross section of the structure (top), plan view of the structure (above).

Fig 4. Assembly on site.

SARA (Switch Activated Response Algorithm)
Felix Dodd

SARA is the prototype for a stable structure that can readily deploy. It is a dynamic space frame with a geometry that generates a movement akin to that of a tongue.

This structure consists of pulsing nickel–titanium wires and rigid aluminium segments individually connected to a source of energy (electricity). Movement is actuated by the change in length of nickel–titanium wire that occurs when a small electronic pulse raises its temperature. The cellular nature of the prototype means that it has the potential to be expanded on an infinite scale.

Each cell can be individually addressed by a microprocessor control system, allowing programmes to manifest as a 1:1 binary mapping. The result is a model of a programmable data structure that can reconfigure its own (data) space.

This project was tutored by Pete Silver and Stephen Gage in Unit 14 at the Bartlett School of Architecture, University College London (UCL), and was a continuation of a groundbreaking and scientific line of research established by John Frazer at the Architectural Association, London, in the 1990s.

Fig 1. SARA prototype displayed at the Bartlett UCL exhibition (1995).

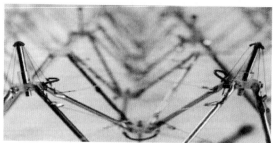

Fig 2. Components that trigger motion.

TENSEGRITY

Tensegrity is a structural principle based on a set of discontinuous components in compression that interacts with a set of continuous tensile elements which are prestressed, thus generating stiffness in the structure and creating a stable volume in space. Therefore, tensegrity can produce structures that are minimal and lightweight.

The term 'tensegrity' was conceived by Richard Buckminster Fuller in 1962, as a combination of the words 'tensile' and 'integrity'. However, the origin of tensegrity structures can be traced much further back.

Tensile concepts were used centuries ago in suspension bridges. The oldest example still in use today is the An-Lan Bridge in Kuanshien, China, which dates from approximately 300 AD (Gómez Jáuregui, 2004, p20). Hoop nets for fishing, which have a tubular shape, are even earlier samples of 'floating compression' elements connected by tensile nets (Silver and McLean, 2013, p56), these – however – are not prestressed as they need to be hung up in order for the nets to be in tension. In 1921 the Russian Constructivist artist Karl Ioganson made a structure called *Study in Balance*, which bears a resemblance to a tensegrity structure. But it was not until 1948 when the first work that can be described as pure tensegrity was created, the *X-Piece* (Figure 1) by the sculptor Kenneth Snelson.

What differentiates Snelson's *X-Piece* from all other tensile structures is that his sculpture is in a constant state of prestress. A structure is prestressed when all its members are always in tension or compression, independently of any external force or input.

Making a tensegrity system deployable has been considered extremely difficult to achieve in practice because it can be unstable and its elements can be entangled. In an interview in 2006 Dr Zhong You suggested that the applications of such systems are limited due to the difficulty of controlling them at every stage of deployment. To date, research papers on this subject have illustrated that the analytical calculations needed are very similar to those of other deployables. While this makes it possible to analyse them mathematically, it does not consider the practical problems of deploying a tensegrity structure.

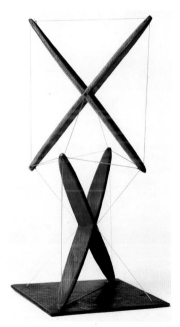

Fig 1. *X-Piece* by Kenneth Snelson (1948).

Examining how to make tensegrity structures deploy, Gunnar Tibert (2002) writes: 'From the deployable structures point of view, tensegrity structures are very interesting since the compressive elements are disjointed. This provides the possibility to fold these members and hence the structure can be compactly stowed.' The versatility and lightness of these structures make them an intriguing geometrical model to study for their potential applications in the aerospace industry. Furthermore, they present unique qualities that may be attractive to designers.

What follows is a series of deployable tensegrity structures that have been developed for applications in space.

Fig 2. Snelson with a double planar structure (1961).

Fig 3. 'Easy-K Installation' by Kenneth Snelson in Arnhem, Holland, 1970.

Four-Stage Mast and Bi-Stable Tube Hinge
Gunnar Tibert and Sergio Pellegrino

This study of deployable tensegrity masts is based on Kenneth
Snelson's mast configuration with three struts per stage. Snelson's
patent *Continuous tension, discontinuous compression structures*
(1965) describes the method of constructing complex large
tensegrity structures from basic modules. Figure 1 illustrates a
three-stage mast that is formed from basic tensegrity modules,
each made with three struts. The modules are then assembled one
on top of the other, with every second module rotated clockwise.
In order to form a stable mast, the cables of the bases are replaced
by saddle cables, and, finally, diagonal cables are added in order
to tension the structure.

A bi-stable tube hinge (BRC tube; see p66) is used for the strut
deployment. Due to the tube's special composite qualities, just a
small amount of energy is required to move it from the rolled-up
to the straight position.

The resulting four-stage mast with bi-stable tube hinges is made of
solid aluminium rods 6.35 millimetres (0.25 inches) in diameter, and
the mast can be folded by hand due to the bi-stability of the hinges.

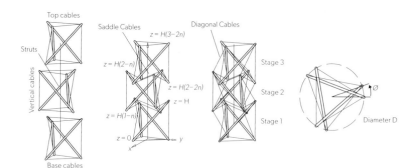

Fig 1. Basic tensegrity modules forming
a three-stage mast.

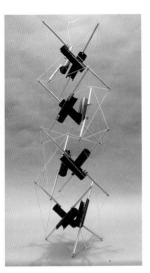

Fig 2–3. Deployable four-stage mast with bi-stable tube hinges.

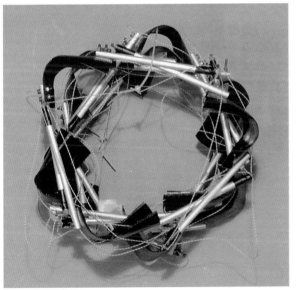

Fig 4. Plan view of stowed four-stage mast.

Eight-Stage Mast
Gunnar Tibert and Sergio Pellegrino

This mast is also based on Kenneth Snelson's idea of constructing complex large tensegrity structures from basic modules, each with three struts per stage.

The aluminium struts of the mast are joined with self-deployable tape-spring hinges. Two 19-millimetre-wide (0.7-inch-wide) tape-springs are bolted to the aluminium tubes with their concave sides facing each other (figure 2). In order to keep the struts in the packaged configuration the mast has to be kept in a canister (figure 1).

To control and to trigger the deployment of the mast, a motorized telescopic aluminium rod is placed through the base of the canister and is connected to the top of the mast through three key nodes. Figures 3 to 5 show the deployment of the mast. One of the cables of the base could extend during deployment to allow all the tape-spring hinges to deploy. This cable would then be shortened by a motorized turnbuckle; only then is the mast fully prestressed.

Fig 1. Front view of the deployable eight-stage mast stowed in a canister.

Fig 2. Top view of the deployable eight-stage mast stowed in a canister.

Fig 3–5. Deployment sequence of the eight-stage mast.

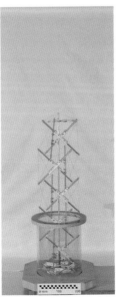
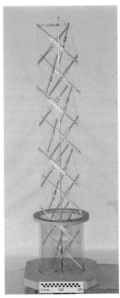

Axi-Symmetric Reflector Antenna
Gunnar Tibert and Sergio Pellegrino

This design principle for a deployable tensegrity antenna for space applications is based on quasi-geodesic nets from the AstroMesh concept and a hexagonal tensegrity module.

The AstroMesh antenna concept uses nets with triangular bands that would follow the geodesic lines of the surface, but that would mean that the nodes of the geodesic lines would not always coincide with the boundary. Therefore, a quasi-geodesic net, known as a geotensoid, is used instead of a true geodesic one (figure 1).

The geotensoid net is assembled on a module based on a hexagonal tensegrity structure.

Figure 2 shows a regular hexagonal tensegrity module, which has 12 joints and 24 bars (the term 'bars' here refers to both tension and compression members). By adding two central joints that connect to the top and bottom hexagons, and are not coplanar with them, the original module is stiffened. Figure 3 shows the resulting modified module, which has 14 joints and 37 bars. However, in order for this structure to be fully prestressed the top hexagon must be rotated slightly clockwise.

Therefore, the resulting structure has six compression members and the rest of the bars are cables. If the compression members are made of collapsible struts then the structure can be easily folded and deployed.

The success of the mechanism relies entirely on the way in which the struts deploy. After several demonstration models were produced, it was found that the telescopic struts were the most promising solution.

The investigation with telescopic struts used the shafts of six identical umbrellas made of telescopic struts 0.46 metres (1.5 feet) in length (figure 4). Figures 5 to 8 show the model suspended by a fishing line to simulate an actual folding. A motor controls the struts in order to achieve a synchronized deployment and prevent any of them from deploying separately at different times.

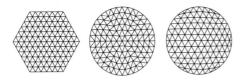

Fig 1. Nets of six rings ('rings' refers to sets of concentric triangles): hexagonal array of equilateral triangles (left); equally spaced concentric circles of triangles (centre); nodes adjusted to achieve a quasi-geodesic arrangement, known as a geotensoid (right).

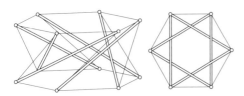

Fig 2. Regular hexagonal tensegrity module: three-dimensional view (left) and top view (right).

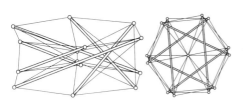

Fig 3. Hexagonal tensegrity module stiffened with central joints and with top hexagon rotated slightly: three-dimensional view (left) and top view (right).

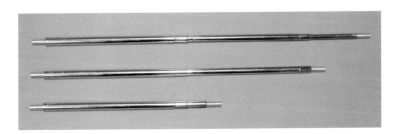

Fig 4. Deployment of telescopic strut.

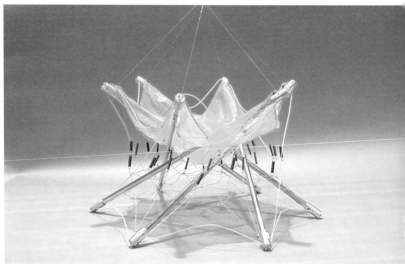

Fig 5–8. Deployment simulation of the antenna with telescopic struts.

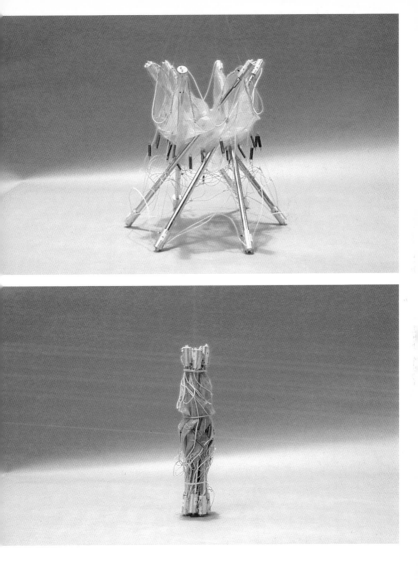

GENERATIVE
TECHNIQUE

3.1 / GENERATIVE TECHNIQUE / ORIGAMI-PAPER PLEAT

Origami and paper pleating techniques are one of the conceptual design approaches from which deployables can be developed. Concepts are explored through paper maquettes, although they may not always be worked up into fully resolved structures.

Origami derives from the Japanese words *ori* ('folding') and *kami* ('paper'). Origami is the ancient Japanese art of transforming a flat sheet of paper into a sculpture or shape. In essence, a two-dimensional object is transformed into a three-dimensional one by a series of folds only. These folds convert the paper object into a new entity with surprising strength and kinetic properties.

Paper gluing or cutting, or assemblages of paper cuts, are not defined as origami but are also explored as 'paper pleats'.

The earliest recorded reference to paper fold studies is probably that of students of Josef Albers in the German design school the Bauhaus in 1927–28 (Wingler, 1969). One of their paper models is quite similar, if not identical, to the well-known Miura-Ori fold, which is believed to derive from the ancient art of origami, and was established by the astrophysicist Koryo Miura in his papers given at the IASS (International Association for Shell and Spatial Structures) Symposium in 1970.

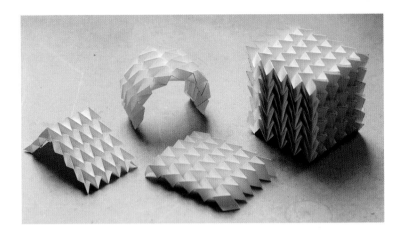

Fig 1. A selection of folded Miura geometries by Mark Schenk. Left to right: angled sheet; continuously transversely curved; planar sheet; stacked set of sheets.

In the 1960s the geometrist, artist and computer scientist Ron Resch conducted relevant studies of deployable origami structures not just in small conceptual models, but also in surprisingly large-scale ones.

Today, applications of deployable origami and paper fold concepts range from aerospace applications to maps, textiles, kinetic art and sculpture.

The following examples demonstrate the development of some origami and paper pleating techniques into deployable mechanisms or prototypes.

Two-Way-Fold Trusses
Maciej Piekarski

The term two-way-fold deployable here refers to structures that have the ability to deploy in two orthogonal directions and are made of rigid components. Two forms of deployable, realized in built projects, have inspired this study: one-way-fold deployable structures (Venezuelan Pavilion for Expo '92, Seville, designed by Zalewski and Hernandez) and scissor structures (a deployable cover for the San Pablo Swimming Pool, Seville, designed by Félix Escrig, Juan Pérez Valcárcel and José Sanchez; see p78).

Two-way-fold deployable structures combine ease of shaping geometrical forms, compressibility and stiffness.

In this work the construction of such structures takes the form of space trusses. The basic module in the shape analysis is a unit of four parallelograms. The union of identical modules forms a flat structure. If the modules are modified, they can form curved structures. Figure 2 shows two different ways of modifying the basic structure.

Figures 5 and 6 show two different approaches to constructing two-way-fold deployable space trusses. The first one uses hinges to join independent polygonal frames. The second approach uses mobile joints that connect individual bars.

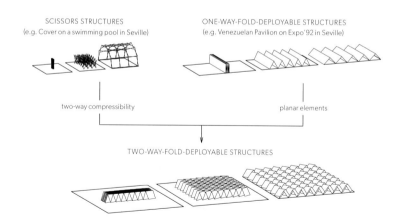

SCISSORS STRUCTURES
(e.g. Cover on a swimming pool in Seville)

ONE-WAY-FOLD-DEPLOYABLE STRUCTURES
(e.g. Venezuelan Pavilion on Expo'92 in Seville)

two-way compressibility

planar elements

TWO-WAY-FOLD-DEPLOYABLE STRUCTURES

Fig 1. Two-way-fold deployable structures in relation to one-way-fold deployable structures and scissor structures.

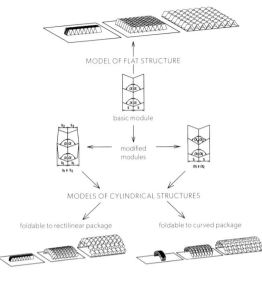

Fig 2. Modifying the geometry of two-way-fold deployable structures.

MODEL OF FLAT STRUCTURE

basic module

modified modules

MODELS OF CYLINDRICAL STRUCTURES

foldable to rectilinear package

foldable to curved package

Fig 3. Phases of transformation called 'states of transformation', with their geodesic lines.

Fig 4. Movable joint prototype.

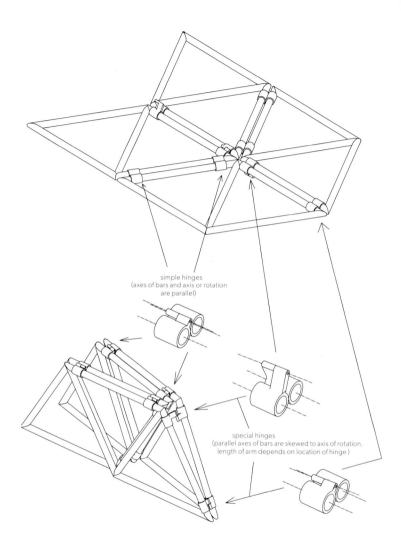

simple hinges
(axes of bars and axis or rotation
are parallel)

special hinges
(parallel axes of bars are skewed to axis of rotation,
length of arm depends on location of hinge)

Fig 5. Principle of operation and construction of
a two-way-fold deployable space truss built from
planar frames connected by hinges.

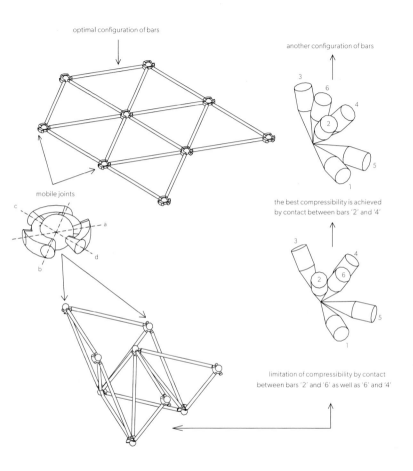

optimal configuration of bars

another configuration of bars

3
6
4
2
5
1

mobile joints

c
a
d
b

the best compressibility is achieved
by contact between bars '2' and '4'

3
4
2
6
5
1

limitation of compressibility by contact
between bars '2' and '6' as well as '6' and '4'

Fig 6. Construction and limitation of compressibility
of two-way-fold deployable space truss built from
bars connected by movable joints.

Rigid-Foldable Thick Origami
Tomohiro Tachi

An ideal, rigid 'zero-thickness' origami is a mathematical model
of a pure origami paper model. This origami model produces
a motion in which the fold lines of the entire structure fold
simultaneously. Its intrinsic geometric configuration allows
it to deploy readily.

Applying this ideal kinetic of origami to architecture is indeed a
challenge. The change of scale requires thicker panels, and that
makes achieving fluid motion a difficult task.

Here the origami scientist Tachi proposes two innovative geometric
methods for applying the ideal kinetic behaviour of zero-thickness
origami to rigid thick foldable origami.

The first uses 'tapered panels'. The proposed kinetic structure
locates the rotational axes of the thick origami to coincide exactly
with the axes of the ideal rigid zero-thickness origami (figure 1).

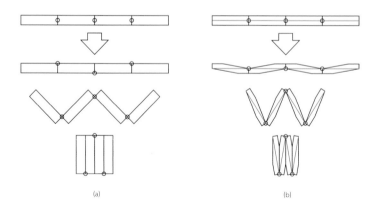

(a)   (b)

Fig 1. Approaches for enabling thick-panel origami.
(Left) axis-shift. (Right) proposed method of tapered
panels by bisecting planes, with the red path
representing the ideal 'zero-thickness' origami.

Fig 2. Trimming the solid facet by bisecting planes of dihedral angles between adjacent facets.

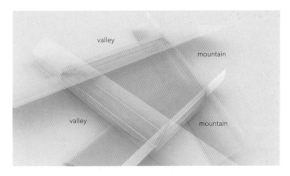

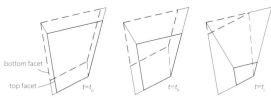

bottom facet
top facet
$t=t_a$ $t=t_b$ $t=t_c$

Fig 3. Proposed method with two constant-thickness panels per facet.

The following describes the procedure for making 'tapered panels'. After an ideal rigid origami without thickness is chosen, in order to thicken it, its surface is offset at both sides with equal distance. In this state the origami cannot be folded as the adjacent facets collide with one another. In order to allow motion, the solid must be 'tapered' by trimming each facet with the bisecting planes of dihedral angles determined by the adjacent facets (figure 2). By establishing the minimum and the maximum folding angles of the thick origami, the structure can move with the ideal kinetic behaviour of zero-thickness origami within that range. Figure 4 shows a quadrilateral-mesh structure with thick tapered panels.

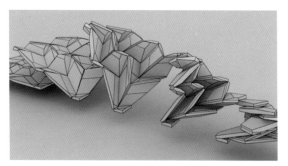

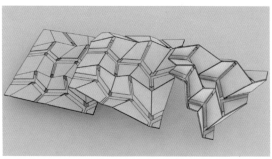

The second method proposed is produced with 'constant-thickness panels'. In essence, it proposes to substitute the tapered facets with two constant-thickness panels that allow the same range of motion described above (figure 3). This method simplifies the fabrication process considerably as the panels can be cut with a regular two-dimensional cutting machine. This configuration produces a series of small apertures at the corners of the panels.

Figure 5 shows the constant-thickness panel version of the quadrilateral-mesh structure. This study has been aided with parametric models, using Grasshopper (a plug-in for Rhinoceros McNeel).

A 2.5 metre x 2.5 metre (8.2 feet x 8.2 feet) prototype of this design (figure 6) has been built with non-mechanical hinges: a strong fabric is sandwiched between two panels that are made of 10-millimetre-thick (0.4-inch-thick) double-walled cardboard.

Fig 6. Prototype built with cloth and cardboard.

Rigid Origami Structures with Vacuumatics

Tomohiro Tachi, Motoi Masubuchi and
Masaaki Iwamoto

This study proposes a novel hybrid structure in which rigid origami
panels are joined to mobile membrane hinges that can be stiffened
in the desired positions using vacuumatics.

Vacuumatics is the process of making rigid a flexible system
of membranes by extracting the air within these membranes.

This hybrid system can be used with any origami pattern, but for
this study a triangular-based regular corrugation (a 'waterbomb';
figure 1) has been chosen, since it can produce a free-form structure.

The rigid origami structure can be built with a double layer
of thick composite panels at either side of a fabric membrane.
In order to achieve the desired mobility, some panels have to
be offset, which results in gaps between the panels on one side
of the structure. This study proposes to place an air-filled chamber
made of breathable material in these gaps on the valley folds
of the corrugated panels, and then to pack the entire origami
structure in an airtight membrane, thus forming a single air
chamber (figures 2–4). Once a vacuum is created, the hinges
bend and stiffen, thus securing the corrugated structure in the
desired position.

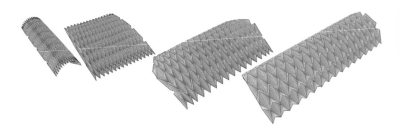

Fig 1. Unfolding sequence of the
'waterbomb' structure.

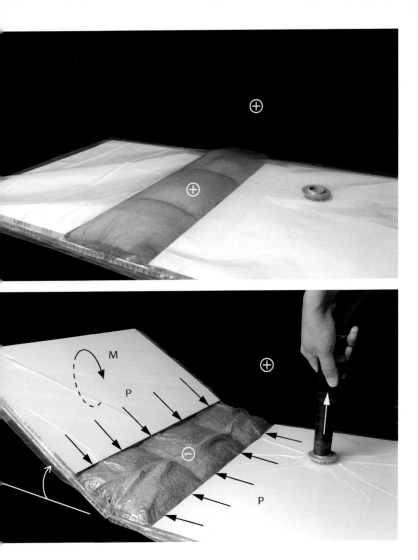

Fig 2–3. Prototype of hinge design
using vacuumatics.

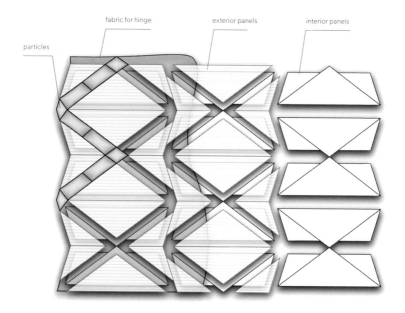

Fig 4. Hinge design diagram.

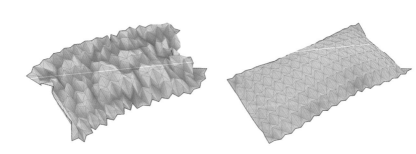

Fig 5. Transformation modes from a flat state: unfavourable (left) and valid (right).

After the structure has been fabricated, a small initial 'bending moment' at each valley fold is applied with the vacuum (Figure 5) in order to fold it out from a flat state. Then the structure is folded by controlling the boundary points fixed on the ground and at the wall (Figure 6). Once on site the structure is deployed in the desired configuration and the membrane hinges are vacuumed completely to stiffen the structure. The structure can be reused by removing the vacuum.

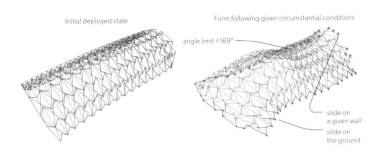

Initial deployed state

Form following given circumstantial conditions

angle limit <169°

slide on a given wall

slide on the ground

Fig 6. Geometric constraints determined by the site.

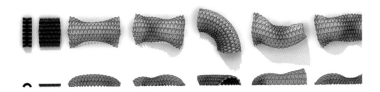

Fig 7. Variational configurations determined by the pinned vertices on the site.

Fig 8. Visualization of the hybrid structure.

Composite Rigid-Foldable Curved Origami Structure

Tomohiro Tachi

Thick-panel rigid origami cannot be folded completely and compactly. This study proposes an alternative that provides a flat, folded three-dimensional origami structure constructed with a tessellation of cellular structures made of thin panels, hence providing the structure with virtual thickness.

The key is using rigid, flat-foldable cylindrical structures with curved folding. Curved folding is a developable surface made of smooth curved creases. Unlike other origami, curved folding allows its bent surface to produce deployment. This results in a simpler fabrication process, due to the reduction of fold lines, while achieving a complex and enticing three-dimensional envelope.

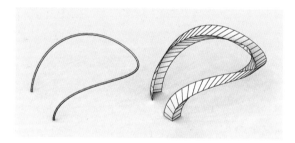

Fig 1. Space curve and curved folding.

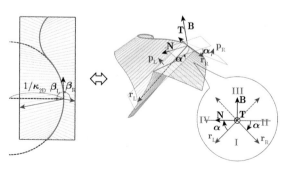

Fig 2. Parameters that determine the crease pattern: top view, perspective and orthogonal projection along vector T. The red line indicates the space curve.

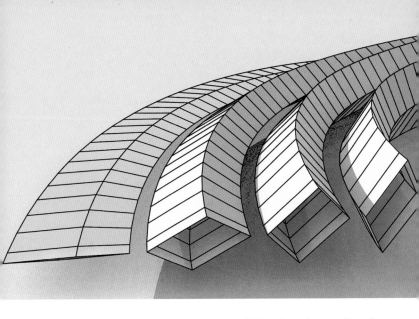

Fig 3. Deployment of the tube from a flat to a curved state.

Curved folding begins with the folding of a single curve. Figure 1 shows a space curve and the curved folding whose crease lies on the space curve.

A space curve can generate a variety of curved folded surfaces. A precise curved folded surface attached to the curve is achieved by defining the folding angle α along the curve.

The angle α is defined by a series of mathematical equations that describe the relationship between the curve's tangent plane and the bi-normal vector B that defines the oscillating plane in which the space curve is contained ('normal' in trigonometry is a vector perpendicular to a plane that defines that plane in space). This is volumetrically explained in figure 2, where the space curve is highlighted in red.

A smooth curve able to generate surfaces that can form a family of tubular structures capable of folding and deploying consistently without bending is selected.

A parametric design system is built using Grasshopper software, which calculates the possible variations of tubular shell structures by determining their generative curve and their continuous folding motion (figure 4). The form of these vaults is manipulated by adjusting the amount of torsion and the proportion of the rectangular section of the tubes. The shell structure is also assessed so that it opens in such way that it is stable on the ground when fully deployed.

A real-life model is shown in figure 5. It was fabricated by first constructing the tube arches by welding two flat sheets and folding them along the creases. The tubes were then joined to form a composite flat-foldable shell.

Fig 4. Vault formed of foldable tubes.

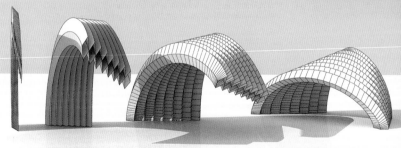

Fig 5. Built prototype.

Rigid Origami Bag

Weina Wu and Zhong You
A solution for folding rigid tall shopping bags © 2011
The Royal Society

This team of engineering scientists has devised a piece of industrial design. This is the first bag made of rigid material that can be folded flat, and potential applications include robotic automated packaging. The conventional shopping bag with a rectangular base, made only in flexible materials such as paper, can be seen in figure 1(a). In 2004 Balkcom et al demonstrated that this folding principle could not be used if the bag was made out of rigid materials. This study proposes a crease pattern that allows a box-shaped bag with a rectangular base, made of rigid materials, to fold flat.

The idea is based on the principle illustrated in figure 1(b). When a bag has a height no greater than half of the depth of the rectangular base, it can fold flat, even if it is made of rigid materials. Thus, the foldability of the bag depends on how the upper and lower parts fold together. Using mathematical and geometrical analyses, which are then tested with simulations and experiments, a novel creasing method is proposed. Figures 2 to 5 show the opening sequence of the proposed bag, which is made of durable paper panels to which thin steel sheets are bonded.

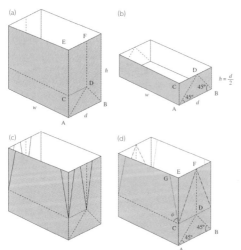

Fig 1. Foldable bag. (a) Standard shopping bag made out of paper; (b) short bag; (c) pattern conjectured by Balkcom et al in 2004; (d) proposed new pattern that allows a rigid bag to fold flat © The Royal Society.

Figs 2–5. Folding sequence of
the proposed bag with new crease.
© Royal Society

3.2 / GENERATIVE TECHNIQUE / BIOMIMETICS

The term biomimetics comes from the Greek words *bios*, which means 'life', and *mimesis*, meaning 'to imitate'.

Biomimetics is the application of methods and systems found in biological systems to the study and design of modern technology. These are not literal copies of biological phenomenology, but abstractions of the principal concepts.

In the 1950s Otto Schmitt conducted probably the first formal doctoral research in the field; he sought to produce a physical device that could mimic the electrical action of a nerve (Vincent et al, 2006). This was a significant attempt to try to enable a function of a living organism in a non-living object. It is thus a subject that requires interdisciplinary thinking and cooperation, or as Schmitt said, 'specializing, or rather, I should say, despecializing into this area of research' (Harkness, 2001).

Velcro, dry adhesive tape, self-cleaning surfaces, and camouflaged garments and equipment are but a few examples of products or principles derived from the study of biomimetics. Although this subject of research is a relatively new one, humans have looked to nature for inspiration for a very long time. One of the earliest examples is the Chinese art of making artificial silk, which began over 3,000 years ago (Vincent et al, 2006).

A contemporary example of architecture derived from biomimetic principles is the 2014 Research Pavilion in the University of Stuttgart by the Institute for Computational Design (ICD) and the Institute of Building Structures and Structural Design (ITKE) in collaboration with palaeontologists from the University of Tübingen. The design of the pavilion is based on the study of the morphology of the abdomen shell of the beetle elytra, known for its strength and lightness and which consists of an array of double-layered modules. Each module derives its strength from a doubly curved concentric structure that forms a double layer made of continuous fibres (trabeculae).

The biomimetic principles of this morphology provide a unique structural logic and strength. This is then translated into a series of principles that enable design and construction on an architectural scale. The key is then to design and manufacture a series of double-layered modules that could be assembled to form the pavilion. Each of these modules is produced by a robotic fabrication process which weaves the double layer from fibre composites filaments; the layer is then submerged into resin to strengthen the filaments further. This process allows a great degree of geometric freedom while reducing considerably the need for formwork.

However, we are here concerned with deployable principles that can be learned from living systems. Those can be mostly seen in two areas, biomimetic principles developed from animals and those developed from plants.

ANIMALS

The combination of morphology and movement in some animals can inspire deployable principles. In some cases the deployable principles are to do with growth, which are non-reversible movements, and in others deployment can occur many times and it is thus a reversible movement.

A key element of biomimetic study is not just to observe independent organs performing a deployable action, but to regard this as the combination of several parameters including a central system that initiates the deployment. This can be especially significant when looking to biomimetics for actuators of deployable mechanisms.

Wing folding in beetles
John H. Brackenbury

Despite having wings, insects spend more time on the ground than in the air. It is thus vital that their delicate wings are stowed away for protection when not in use.

Beetles are particularly interesting due to the morphology of their hindwings, which are the main lift-generating surfaces and are stowed under the forewings. The hindwings are normally much larger than the forewings, and so need to be able to fold.

Far from being smooth, the texture of the insect's wing is usually corrugated along certain longitudinal lines spanning out from the base. These geometrical configurations generate corrugations that impart a radial architecture with potential for fan-wise mobility, which is developed to its fullest extent in the highly pleated hindwing of locusts, crickets and mantids.

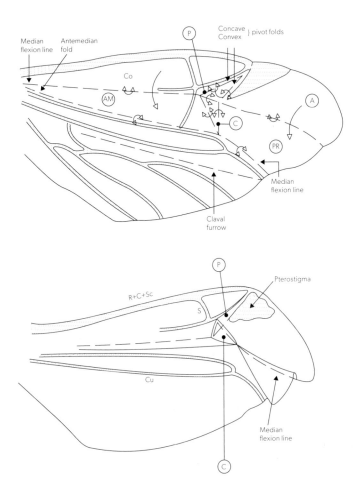

Fig 1. Dorsal view of right wing of Cantharis in fully open and partially folded stage. Main flexion lines are indicated by dashed lines. Curved arrows signify whether the fold line is convex or concave. Circled letters indicate wing areas or plates. Plates: Co – costal; AM – antemedian; P – pivot; C – central; A – apical; PR – principal. Veins: Cu – cubital; R – radial; Sc – subcostal; S – sectoral; M – median.

Concave } pivot folds
Convex }

Median flexion line

Antemedian fold

Co

AM

P

A

C

PR

Median flexion line

Claval furrow

P

R+C+Sc

S

Pterostigma

Cu

Median flexion line

C

Fig 2. Wing folding occurs by elastic stiffening around the flexion lines in the wasp-beetle Clytus. The shaded area is the helical band that crosses three successive concave fold lines.

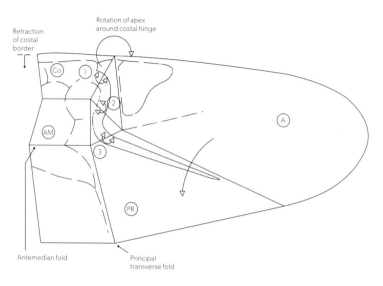

Retraction of costal border

Rotation of apex around costal hinge

Co

AM

A

PR

Antemedian fold

Principal transverse fold

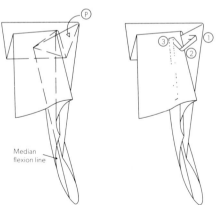

P

Median flexion line

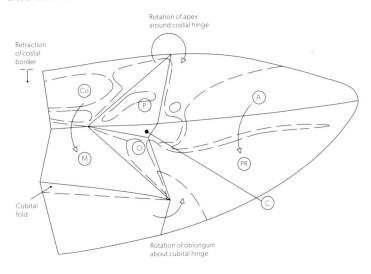

Fig 3. Wing folding pattern in the carabid *Pterostichus*.

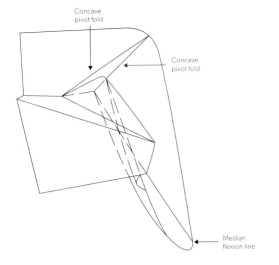

PLANTS

The morphology and movement of some plants can inspire biomimetic deployable principles, which can also involve reversible and non-reversible movements. In some cases the deployment is activated by an external force, such as a bird landing on a flower. This mechanism can be found in the *Strelitzia reginae*, the abstraction of which is one of the case studies that follow.

Geometry of unfolding tree leaves
H. Kobayashi, B. Kresling and J. F. V. Vincent

Leaves of hornbeam and beech trees have a consistent folding pattern that allows numerical study and modelling abstraction of deployable flat planes made of parallel folds based on the Miura-Ori fold (see p104).

A leaf has a straight primary central vein that divides symmetrically an array of parallel secondary veins creating a corrugated surface. In both hornbeam and beech leaves the angle between the main vein and secondary veins increases gradually from 30 to 50 degrees towards the petiole (stalk) of the leaf; its average angle is 40 degrees. This simple and pure geometrical arrangement may be related to the leaf's biological functions of nutrient absorption and support.

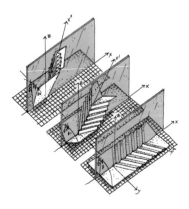

Fig 1. Opening of a corrugated paper model of a leaf.
© The Royal Society

Fig 2. Hornbeam branch that displays the opening sequence of the corrugated leaves (opposite).

Two half-leaf models with different vein angles have been simulated and illustrated in a graph (figure 3), one with an angle of 30 degrees and another with an angle of 85 degrees. Although the models are identical when fully unfolded, the unfolding process of each is significantly different. The leaf with the 30-degree vein angle deploys gradually as the leaf unfolds and achieves a relatively large deployment in the early stages of unfolding. The other elongates dramatically in the final stages of deployment. Although both require more energy in the later stages of deployment, the larger the vein angle, the more energy will be required to fully unfold the leaf, while allowing a more efficient packaging in the initial stages.

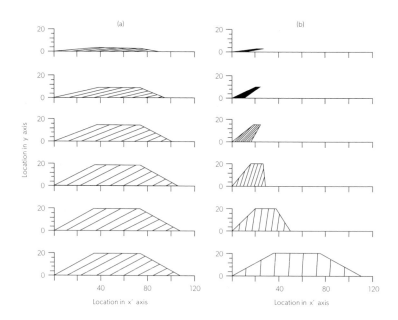

Fig 3. Unfolding process of half-leaf paper models with a vein angle of (a) 30 degrees and (b) 85 degrees.
© The Royal Society

Elastic Kinematics Concepts for Adaptive Shading Systems

Simon Schleicher, Julian Lienhard, Simon Poppinga,
Tom Masselter, Thomas Speck, Jan Knippers and
Markus Milwich

This multidisciplinary collaboration of biologists, engineers and architects has formulated a novel elastic mechanism inspired by plant biomimetics that can be used as shading for facades. It does not have the constraints of current rigid shading components and has no hinges or joints, making it ideal for free-form facades.

Plants have special anatomical and morphological characteristics that allow

them to bend with a high degree of flexibility while retaining their structural stability. Although this is quite common in nature, the notion of pliable principles is rare in architectural structures.

The following two case studies, one of a flower opening and the other of a leaf folding, will test their complex reversible elastic deformations and their potential application for architectural concepts.

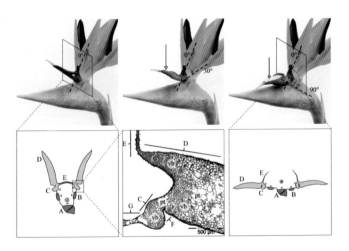

Fig 1. Photos and cross section of the elastic deformation of *Strelitzia reginae*. © IOPscience 2011 Bioinspir. Biomim. 6 045001

Abstraction of the Elastic Kinematics of *Strelitzia reginae* (Flectofin®)

This case study examines the biological deformation of the *Strelitzia reginae* (a flower also known as the bird of paradise; figure 1), which is then abstracted to a pliable structure and a flap named Flectofin® (figure 2).

The bird of paradise is ornithophilous, which means that birds transfer the pollen from one flower to another, leading to reproduction. In order to reach the nectar, the birds land on the flower perch, made of two jointed petals or flaps. The weight of the bird causes the petals to bend downwards and sideways, revealing the anthers and the style (male and female sexual organs), while the pollen sticks to the bird. Once the bird leaves the flower, the open perch returns to its original closed state due to its elastic morphology.

Figure 1 shows the above principle and its morphology. The cross section of the perch reveals that there are three lateral reinforcing ribs at both sides (A, B and C), connected with a thin flexible lamina (E). The lower ribs on both sides are fused together (A) and the top ribs merge into a large flap lamina at either side (D and E) that overlaps, covering the anthers. This mechanism is reversible and durable; it is reliable enough to perform 3,000 cycles without signs of deterioration.

A simulation of the kinematic principles described above uses various models, physical and digital, in which a thin flap is connected perpendicularly along its length to a cantilevered backbone. Bending the backbone slightly will trigger torsional buckling, forcing the flap to bend unsymmetrically: a principle now patented as Flectofin® (figure 2).

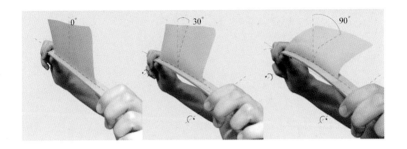

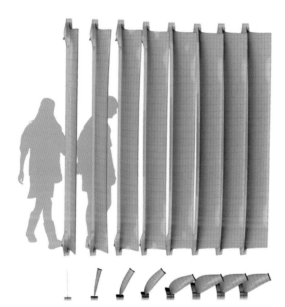

Fig 2. Basic physical model of Flectofin® principle (opposite above). © IOPscience 2011 Bioinspir. Biomim. 6 045001

Fig 3. Adjustable shading made with fins.

A key issue is whether the concept can be used on an architectural scale. Upscaling depends on the ratio of geometrical to elastic stiffnesses. The latter is defined by material properties, thus upscaling is usually much easier than downscaling, although it involves redefining the parameters of the material. In the light of this, the Flectofin® principle has been validated for a distance ranging from 0.2 metres (0.65 feet) to 14 metres (46 feet). A 1:1 scale prototype made out of glass-fibre reinforced plastic (figure 4) for exterior fins has been built with a height of 2 metres (6.6 feet), width of 0.25 metres (0.8 feet) and thickness of 2 millimetres (0.07 inches).

Fig 4. Full-scale mock-up of three 2-metre-high (6.6-feet-high) double Flectofin® lamellas in parallel arrangement.

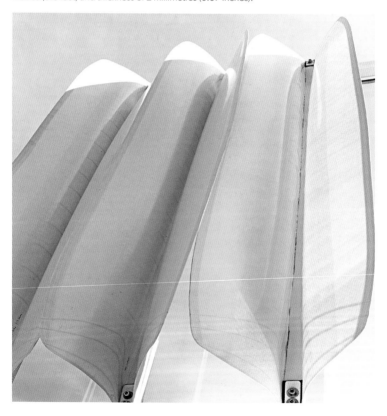

Abstraction of the Curved-Line Folding Elastic Kinematics of *Aldrovanda Vesiculosa*

This study intends to gain a better understanding of the curved-line folding elastic kinematics of *Aldrovanda vesiculosa*, also known as the waterwheel plant, and to compare it with the Flectofin® principle.

Aldrovanda vesiculosa is a carnivorous, free-floating aquatic plant with a fascinating trap mechanism that captures small aquatic invertebrates. The traps are arranged in whorls around its central free-floating stem (figure 5). The trap is approximately 5 millimetres (0.2 inches) long and consists of two lobes that fold together along the midrib, forming a snap-trap (figure 6). When the sensory hairs of the trap mechanism are stimulated by the prey, the trap-lobes close instantly. While the trap closes in a few milliseconds – quite impressive considering that it is underwater – it takes up to half an hour to reopen. This trap is another example of reversible elastic surface deformations but with an additional feature, its curved-line folding geometry.

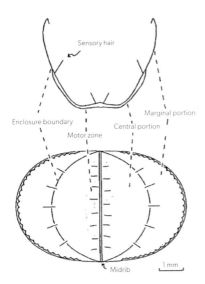

Fig 5. Carnivorous plant, *Aldrovanda vesiculosa*, with traps at the end of the stems (overleaf).

Fig 6. Cross section and plan of the trap of the *Aldrovanda vesiculosa*.

The abstraction of the elastic kinematics of *Aldrovanda vesiculosa* is highly complex. A very small linear displacement actuates the complex deformation of multiple surfaces. In order to understand how the patterns deform, a Rigid Origami Simulator software is used. The biological lobe is converted in a quad-dominant mesh with planar faces so as to study the pattern.

Various simulations of the pattern kinematics use FEM simulations with a laminate thickness of 10 millimetres (0.4 inches) in the central portion, 5 millimetres (0.2 inches) in the lobes of the marginal portion, and a curved line of 1 millimetre (0.04 inches) to allow motion. The pattern is further improved by the addition of rib stiffenings along the curved-line bending zone as well as in the midrib (figure 8).

This novel bio-inspired pliable shading system is ideal for architectural applications with double-curved, free-form geometries.

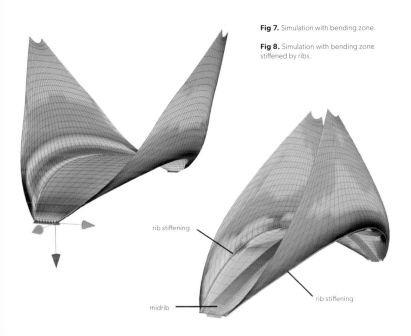

Fig 7. Simulation with bending zone.

Fig 8. Simulation with bending zone stiffened by ribs.

rib stiffening

rib stiffening

midrib

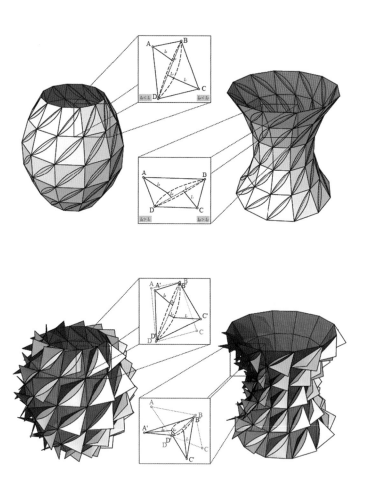

Figs 9–10. Parametric simulations of curved-line folding modules on synclastic and anticlastic geometries.

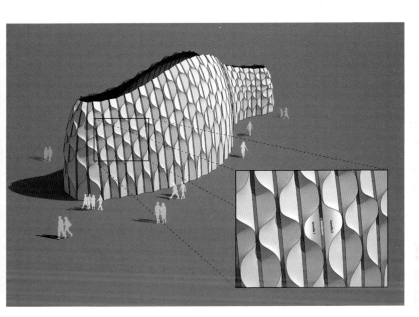

Fig 11. Implementation of Flectofin®
as a parametric component on a
free-form façade.

SYNTEGRATION

4.1 / SYNTEGRATION / RESPONSIVENESS

A kinetic structure can be programmed with a particular set of instructions, or it can be connected to sensors that react when certain changes occur naturally in the environment around it (for example daylight and motion).

Most deployable structures seem to be operated manually in reaction to weather conditions (for example daylight or rain), or to expand a flexible space and thus allow architecture to adapt to multiple changes in the environment. But responsive parameters can be used to enable a deployable structure to enter into a dialogue with life around it.

A project that illustrates this potential is the Aegis Hyposurface, designed by dECOi, an architectural practice founded by Mark Goulthorpe, and built in 2001. The project is essentially a wall, but its surface – constructed as a faceted set of metallic triangles – can be completely reconfigured in response to real-time stimuli around it, including that of people nearby. The triangles incorporate more than 1,000 pneumatic pistons that can create waves, allowing patterns of motion to be sent through the entire surface.

The Aegis Hyposurface is not a deployable structure. Although it shares an ability to reconfigure itself, every panel of it is controlled completely independently. Furthermore, it does not have the ability to be packaged into a substantially different state, and its geometry, although it is topologically connected, is not interdependent physically. Its geometry is, however, digitally interconnected.

The Aegis Hyposurface does, however, raise an interesting conceptual proposition. The idea that a structure can react to perceived stimuli could be transferred to a deployable. This could mean that, in addition to fulfilling functional requirements, a deployable structure could become an expressively responsive entity.

A prototype of this idea was developed in John Frazer's unit at the Architectural Association, London, in 1993 (Frazer, 1995, p97). The prototype was an 'interactive skin', essentially a wall, that responds to various stimuli. Pete Silver offers a vivid window on an important moment when architects collaborated with cybernetitian and psychologist Gordon Pask, during his long-term alliance with John Frazer's unit:

'An increasing fascination with machine logic, machine intelligence and electronic control was driving all of us into the information age. Architecture could evolve, could sense and respond, could become intelligent and alive ...' (1997)

Gordon Pask describes Frazer's work as follows:

'The fundamental thesis is that of architecture as a living, evolving thing. ... The role of the architect here, I think, is not so much to design a building or a city as to catalyse them; to act that they may evolve.' (Pask, 1995, pp6 and 7)

4.2 / SYNTEGRATION / GEOMETRIC SYNTEGRATION

On the quest to decipher a classification system and to present a wide variety of deployable principles with potential application in architecture and design, this book has linked work from such disparate disciplines that it would seem to contradict today's practice methodology, which is driven towards specialization.

'… Society operates on the theory that specialization is the key to success, not realizing that specialization precludes comprehensive thinking.'

BUCKMINSTER FULLER, 1969

Buckminster Fuller did indeed understand the complexity and challenges of a profession – architecture – that is increasingly becoming more fragmented as it navigates against the tide of specialization. Today's architectural practice is dissected from all angles, from pure architectural theorists to pragmatist approaches, and its specializations range from design, geometry, drawing and painting, to material science, structural engineering, environmental engineering, history, computer science, surveying, landscape design, interior design, industrial design, model making, building and architectural psychology. … The list goes on. The more we gain an understanding of our world, the more specialities arise, and the more specialized the specialities become.

It is thus refreshing to find a speciality – that of deployable structures – that does not allow itself to be secluded, but

Fig 1. Fractional view of Geometry Machine by Esther Rivas Adrover, Crosby Beach, Liverpool.

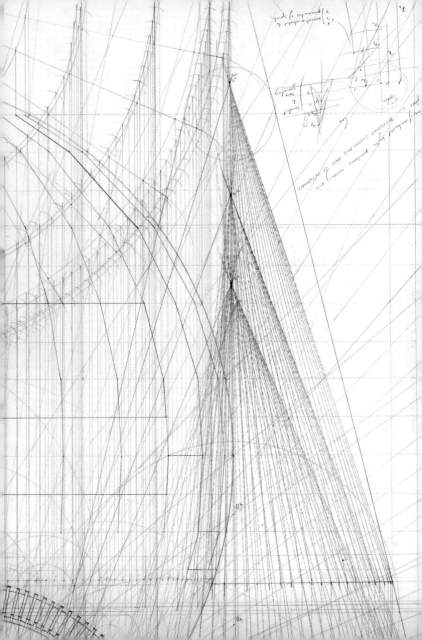

that spreads across unpredictable territories, and seeks to unify knowledge from apparently disparate disciplines.

Following Fuller, I would argue that 'specialization *can* preclude comprehensive thinking' and that much could be gained from paying equal attention to what I denominate 'syntegration': that is to say, 'synergetic integration'. When we interlink knowledge and research from various disciplines, truly meaningful ideas can emerge.

In his essay 'The Architecture of Life' (1998), Donald E. Ingber explains that '… my studies of cell biology and also of sculpture led me to realize that the question of how living things form has less to do with chemical composition than with architecture'. The premise that architectural studies can be useful even at the cellular and molecular level is the ultimate evidence of the syntegration that connects architecture with all life.

Syntegration principles enable architecture to be a complex living system, and, borrowing from Ingber, 'understanding what the parts of a complex machine are made of … does little to explain how the whole system works'. Syntegration can make specialization more rich and dynamic. By looking outside a single window, incongruous clues can be found to solve one given problem. And in turn specialization can provide vital nutrients to syntegration.

The geometry of deployable systems also seems to follow from nature's patterns, such as spirals, hexagons and spheres, which are recurrent at the micro and macro scales. Although these are born in our minds as symmetrical geometries, this is only the origin of their journey. From order to chaos we will no doubt find them in intermediate unexpected states. Principles of deployable inflatable domes will create irregular organic formations. Scissor deployables may not just construct regular forms but radical asynchronic tectonics. Deployable solid surfaces will find ways to deploy their plates not just in perfect symmetry, but in an apparently random order. Deployable structures could help us to understand an intrinsic order that we may find in an apparent chaos.

These geometric formations are but one frame in the great animation of life. For billions of years nature has been evolving deployable systems, such as the growth of leaves or the opening of a beetle's wings. We also know that the architectural principles of Buckminster Fuller's deployable tensegrity geodesic spheres and Snelson's sculptures appear to even explain how water molecules are structured. In a continuous cycle, we learn deployable geometrical concepts from nature, and deployable geometric principles help us to understand nature.

The geometric syntegration qualities of deployables seem to allow for almost infinite applications.

If there are such beautiful underlying deployable geometries that are now being discovered and analysed, one can only begin to imagine what wonders nature retains, unearthed, in store, for us.

'It should not be hard for you to stop sometimes and look into the stains of walls, or ashes of a fire, or clouds, or mud or like places, in which ... you may find really marvellous ideas.'

LEONARDO DA VINCI, CODEX ATLANTICUS; REPRO. IN WHITE, 2000

SOURCES

Web

www.ajtensile.co.uk
http://architecturemyart.blogspot.com/2013/01/
  7-principles-of-home-interior-design.html
www.atk.com/products-services/telescoping-boom/
www.bfi.org/domes
www.birdsportchmouthrussum.com/bpr/pr-coolhurst.html
www.civ.eng.cam.ac.uk/dsl/index_2007.html
www.civil.eng.ox.ac.uk/people/zy/research/
  publications.html
http://collection.cooperhewitt.org/objects/18699461/
www.docomomo-us.org/register/fiche/mellon_arena
http://drum.lib.umd.edu//handle/1903/1788
www.element-energy.co.uk/services/engineering-
  solutions/cfd/aerostat-for-the-commonwealth-games/
http://erikdemaine.org/curved/history/
www.flanaganlawrence.com/home/soundforms#grid
www.grunch.net/snelson/rmoto.html
www.heatherwick.com/index.php?option
  =com_content&task=view&id=19&Itemid=48
www.hoberman.com/popup.html
http://icps.proboards.com/
www.kennethsnelson.net/KennethSnelson_Art_
  And_Ideas.pdf
www.lindstrandtech.com/
www.markschenk.com/research/
www.miura-ori.com/English/e-index.html
www.miura-ori.com/English/e-what.html
www.nasa.gov/mission_pages/shuttle/shuttlemissions/
  sts131/launch/131mission_overview.html
www.nervionaldia.com/el-psoe-critica-que-la-piscina-
  de-san-pablo-construida-en-1997-siga-cerrada/
www.northropgrumman.com/BusinessVentures/
  AstroAerospace/Pages/History.aspx
www.northropgrumman.com/BusinessVentures/
  AstroAerospace/Products/Documents/pageDocs/
  STEM_Hardware_Programs.pdf
www.origami-resource-center.com/origami-science.html
www.oxfordspacestructures.com/spacecot
www.patentsmalaysia.com/2010/01/origami-patents.html
www.pellegrino.caltech.edu/PUBLICATIONS/Arm%20
  development_%20review%20of%20existing%20
  technologies%202001.pdf
www.perezpinero.org/
www.pghmodern.org/content/civic-arena
www.rajko.net/judit/juditsite.swf
http://rolatube.com/
www.sial.rmit.edu.au/Projects/Aegis_Hyposurface.php
www.soundforms.co.uk/#ad-image-0
www.spiegel.de/international/zeitgeist/how-
  did-egyptian-folding-chairs-end-up-in-northern-
  germany-a-830958.html
http://thomasguild.blogspot.co.uk/2011/12/
  medieval-folding-chairs.html
www.tsg.ne.jp/TT/cg/index.html
http://vimeo.com/36122966
webcache.googleusercontent.com/search?q=cache:_
  DpfGNewSisJ:www-civ.eng.cam.ac.uk/dsl/research/
  ki206/bistable.html+&cd=5&hl=en&ct=clnk&gl=uk
http://xy2.org/lenka/TurinKha.html
www.west8.nl/W8_Archives/archive.html
www.youtube.com/watch?v=DmZLuyK3xS0
www.youtube.com/watch?v=N1oVXgvr9DE&feature=relmfu
www.youtube.com/watch?v=QvHpOmD8Zlg
www.youtube.com/watch?v=uSSM8AchmQg
www.youtube.com/watch?v=zyZZktZgamI
http://nmp.jpl.nasa.gov/st8/tech/sailmast_tech3.html
www.dezeen.com/2014/06/26/icd-itke-pavilion-
  beetle-shells-university-of-stuttgart/

Books

Baldwin, J., *Bucky Works: Buckminster Fuller's Ideas for Today*. John Wiley & Sons, London, 1996.

Bini, Dante, *Building with Air*. Bibliotheque McLean, London, 2014.

Buckminster Fuller, R (series editor: Snyder, Jaime), *Operating Manual for Spaceship Earth*. Lars Müller Publishers, Zurich, 2008 (first published in 1969).

Escrig, F., and Brebbia, C. A. (eds), 'General Survey of Deployability in Architecture', in *Mobile and Rapidly Assembled Structures*. WIT Press, Southampton, 1996.

Geradin, M., Motro, R., Pellegrino, S., Tarnai, T., and Vincent, J. F. V, *Deployable Structures*, ed Sergio Pellegrino, CISM International Centre for Mechanical Sciences, Springer Vienna, vol 412, 2001.

Gordon Pask.. Frazer, John, *An Evolutionary Architecture*. Architectural Association (Themes VII), London, 1995, pp 6–7.

Calladine, Gantes, C. J. (editor), *Deployable Structures: Analysis and Design*. WIT Press, Southampton, 2001 p 64.

Hoberman, Chuck, 'Expanding Sphere 1988–92 and Iris Dome 1990–94', in Lynn, Greg (ed), *Archaeology of the Digital*. Canadian Centre for Architecture and Sternberg Press, Montreal, 2013.

Hoberman, Chuck, 'Unfolding Architecture' in Lynn, Greg (ed), *Folding in Architecture: Architectural Design*. Wiley-Academy, London, 2004. p 72.

Kelly, Kevin, *Out of Control: The New Biology of Machines, Social Systems, and the Economic World*. Perseus Books, Cambridge, MA, 1994.

Killory, Christine, and Davids, René, *Details in Contemporary Architecture*. AsBuilt, Princeton Architectural Press, New York, 2007, p 170.

McLean, Will, *Quik Build: Adam Kalkin's ABC of Container Architecture*. Bibliotheque McLean, London, 2008, p 37.

Otto, Frei (ed), *Tensile Structures: Design Structure and Calculation of Bldgs. of Cables, Nets and Membranes*. MIT Press, Cambridge, MA, 1973.

Rasch, Bodo, and Otto, Frei, *Finding Form: Towards an Architecture of the Minimal*. Edition Axel Menges, Deutscher Werkbund Bayern, Stuttgart, 2001.

Siegal, Jennifer (ed), *MOBILE: the Art of Portable Architecture*. Princeton Architectural Press, New York, 2002.

Silver, Pete and McLean, Will, *Introduction to Architectural Technology* (second edition). Laurence King Publishing, London, 2013, p 56.

Silver, Pete, McLean, Will, Hardingham, Samantha, and Veglio, Simon, *Fabrication: The Designer's Guide*. Architectural Press, London, 2006.

White, Michael, *Leonardo da Vinci: The First Scientist*. Abacus, London, 2000.

Wingler, Hans M. (trans. Jabs, Wolfgang, and Gilbert, Basil; ed Stein, Joseph), *Bauhaus: Weimar, Dessau, Berlin, Chicago*. MIT Press, Cambridge, MA, and London, 1969, p 435.

De Temmerman, N. (Author, Editor), Brebbia, C. A. (Editor). *Mobile and Rapidly Assembled Structures: IV*. WIT Transactions on the Built Environment, Vrije Universiteit Brussel, Belgium. WIT Press, Southampton, UK, 2014.

Motro René (editor). *An Anthology of Structural Morphology*. World Scientific Publishing, USA & UK, 2009.

Herzog, Thomas and Minke, Gernot. *Pneumatic structures: A handbook for the architect and engineer*. Crosby Lockwood Staples. London, 1977.

Tilder, Lisa and Blostein, Beth (editors). *Design Ecologies. Essays on the Nature of Design*, Princeton Architectural Press, New York, 2010

Symposium Papers

The following papers were published in *IUTAM-IASS Symposium on Deployable Structures: Theory and Applications, Cambridge*, ed S. Pellegrino and S. D. Guest. Kluwer Academic Publishers, Dordrecht, 2000:

Al Khayer, Mohamad and Lalvani, Haresh, 'Scissors-Action Deployables Based on Space-Filling of Polygonal Hyperboloids'.

Brackenbury, J. H., 'Wing Folding in Beetles', p 37.

Britt, Alan L., and Lalvani, Haresh, 'Symmetry as a Basis for Morphological Analysis and Generation of NASA Type Cubic Deployables'.

Kanemitsu, Tomomi (et al.), 'Self-Deployable Antenna Using Centrifugal Force'.

Karni, E., 'Deployable Swimming Pool Enclosures'.

Kawaguchi, K., 'A New Approach to Retractable Membrane Structures', p 193.

Piekarski, Maciej, 'Constructional Solutions for Two-Way-Fold Deployable Space Trusses', p 302.

Rimrott, F. P. J., and Fritzsche, G., 'Fundamentals of Stem Mechanics'.

Other Papers, Journals And Articles

De Focatiis, Davide, 'Deployable Membranes Designed from Folding Tree Leaves', *Philosophical Transactions of the Royal Society A*, vol 373, issue 2035, 2001, pp 227–238.

Silver, Peter, Dodd, Felix, Holdon, Tom, Leung, Chris, and Pletts, Josephine, 'Prototypical Applications of Cybernetic Systems in Architectural Contexts: A Tribute to Gordon Pask', *Kybernetes*, vol 30, nos 7/8, 2001, pp 902–920.

Escrig, Félix, Valcárcel, Juan Pérez, and Sanchez, José, 'Deployable Cover on a Swimming Pool in Seville', *Journal of the International Association for Shell and Spatial Structures*, vol 37, no. 120, 1996.

Goulthorpe, M., 'Aegis Hyposurface Autoplastic to Alloplastic', *Architectural Design: Hypersurface Architecture II*, vol 69, 1999.

Ingber, D. E., 'The Architecture of Life', *Scientific American*, vol 278, no. 1, 1998, pp 48–57.

SOURCES

Jensen, Frank Vadstrup, and Pellegrino, Sergio, 'Arm Development Review of Existing Technologies', Technical report, Cambridge University Department of Engineering, 2001, p 17.

Jensen, Frank Vadstrup, and Pellegrino, Sergio, 'Expandable 'BLOB' Structures', *Journal of the International Association for Shell and Spatial Structures*, vol 46, no. 3, 2005, p 151.

Kassabian, P. E., You, Z., and Pellegrino, S, 'Retractable Roof Structures', *Structures and Buildings*, Proceedings of the Institution of Civil Engineers, vol 134, issue 1, 1999, pp 45–56.

Kobayashi, H., Kresling, B., and Vincent, J. F. V., 'The Geometry of Unfolding Tree Leaves', *Proceedings of the Royal Society B*, vol 256, no. 1391, 1998, pp 147–154

Miura, K., and Pellegrino, S., 'Structural Concepts', 1999 [draft manuscript].

Nishiyama, Yutaka, 'Miura Folding: Applying Origami to Space Exploration', *International Journal of Pure and Applied Mathematics*, vol 79, no. 2, 2012, pp 269–279.

Schleicher, Simon; Lienhard, Julian; Knippers, Jan; Poppinga, Simon; Masselter, Tom; and Speck, Thomas, 'Bio-inspired Kinematics for Adaptive Shading Systems on Free-Form Facades', *Taller, Longer, Lighter – Meeting growing demand with limited resources*, IABSE-IASS 2011 Symposium Report, IABSE Reports, no. 98, London, 2011.

Schleicher, Simon; Lienhard, Julian; Poppinga, Simon; Masselter, Tom; Milwich, Markus; Speck, Thomas, and Knippers, Jan, 'Flectofin: A Hingeless Flapping Mechanism Inspired by Nature', *Bioinspiration & Biomimetics*, vol 6, no. 4, 2011.

Schleicher, Simon; Lienhard, Julian; Poppinga, Simon; Masselter, Tom; Speck, Thomas and Knippers, Jan, 'Adaptive Facade Shading Systems Inspired by Natural Elastic Kinematics', presented at the International Adaptive Architectural Conference IAAC, London, 2011.

Tachi, Tomohiro, 'Rigid-Foldable Thick Origami', paper presented at Fifth International Meeting of Origami Science, Mathematics, and Education, Singapore, July 2010.

Tachi, Tomohiro, Masubuchi, Motoi, and Iwamoto, Masaaki, 'Rigid Origami Structures with Vacuumatics: Geometric Considerations. Research supported by JST PRESTO', *Proceedings of the IASs–APCS Symposium 2012: From Spatial Structures to Space Structures*, Seoul, 2011.

Wu, Weina, and You, Zhong, 'A Solution for Folding Rigid Tall Shopping Bags', *Proceedings of the Royal Society A*, 2011.

You, Zhong, and Chen, Yan, 'On Mobile Assemblies of Bennett Linkages', *Proceedings of the Royal Society A*, vol 464, issue 2093, 2008, pp 1275–1293.

Hanaor, A. and Levy R.. 'Evaluation of Deployable Structures for Space Enclosures', *International Journal of Space Structures*. Vol 16, No. 4, 2001, pp 221–229.

Harkness, J. M., 'A lifetime of connections: Otto Herbert Schmitt, 1913–1998', *Physics in Perspective*, vol 4, issue 4, 2002, pp 456–490.

F. V. Vincent, Julian; Bogatyreva, Olga A.; Bogatyrev, Nikolaj R.; Bowyer, Adrian and Pahl, Anja-Karina. 'Biomimetics: its practice and theory', *Journal of the Royal Society Interface*, vol 3, 2006, pp 471–482. Published online: http://rsif.royalsocietypublishing.org/content/3/9/471.full.pdf+html [accessed 14.01.15].'

Chi, Jung Yun and Pauletti, Ruy Marcelo de Oliveira. An outline of the evolution of pneumatic structures'. Faculty of Architecture and Urban Planning of the University of São Paulo and Polytechnic School of the University de São Paulo, 2005. Published online: http://www.lmc.ep.usp.br/people/pauletti/Publicacoes_arquivos/Chi-and-Pauletti.Pdf [accessed 14.01.15].

Doctoral Theses

Jensen, Frank Vadstrup, 'Cover Elements for Retractable Roof Structures'. Department of Engineering, Darwin College, University of Cambridge, 2001.

Schenk, Mark, 'Folded Shell Structures'. Clare College, University of Cambridge, 2011, p 32.

Tibert, Gunnar, 'Deployable Tensegrity Structures for Space Applications'. Department of Engineering, University of Cambridge, and Royal Institute of Technology, Stockholm, 2002, pp 1, 2 and 13.

Kuribayashi, Kaori. 'A Novel Foldable Stent Graft'. St. Catherine's College. Department of Engineering Science at University of Oxford. 2004.

Rhode-Barbarigos, Landolf-Giosef-Anastasios.'An Active Deployable Tensegrity Structure'. À La Faculté De L'environnement Naturel, Architectural Et Construit Laboratoire D'informatique Et De Mécanique Appliquées À La Construction Programme Doctoral En Structures. École Polytechnique Fédérale De Lausanne. Suisse. 2012.

Theses

Dora Adler, Esther, 'A New Unity! The Art and Pedagogy of Josef Albers'. Master of Arts thesis in Art, History and Archaeology, University of Maryland, 2004.

Gómez Jáuregui, Valentín, 'Tensegrity Structures and their Application to Architecture'. School of Architecture, Queen's University, Belfast, 2004. p 20.

Patents

Chen, Yan, and You, Zhong, *Deployable Structure*. US Patent Number: 6,941,704 B2, 2005.

Hoberman, Charles, *Radial Expansion/Retraction Truss Structures*. US Patent Number: 5,024,031.,1991.

Pérez Piñero, Emilio, *Three-dimensional Reticular Structure*. Patent 3,185,164, 25 May 1965.

Snelson, Kenneth D., *Continuous Tension, Discontinuous Compression Structures*. US Patent Number: 3,169,611, 1965.

Conferences

Flanagan Lawrence, 'Soundforms: A Paper on the Design, Development and Fabrication of a 1:1 Scale Mobile Acoustic Performance Shell Prototype. Piano Test, C. Nick Guttridge, 2012'. Prototyping Architecture: International Conference, London, 21–23 February 2013.

Jensen, Frank Vadstrup, and Pellegrino, Sergio, 'Expandable Structures formed by Hinged Plates'. Department of Engineering, University of Cambridge, Fifth International Conference on Space Structures, University of Surrey, 19–21 August 2002.

Miura, Koryo, and Tachi, Tomohiro, 'Synthesis of Rigid-Foldable Cylindrical Polyhedra'. Symmetry: Art and Science, Gmünd, Austria 23–28 August 2010.

Tachi, Tomohiro, 'Composite Rigid-Foldable Curved Origami Structure'. Proceedings of the First Conference, Transformables 2013, in Honour of Emilio Perez Piñero, School of Architecture, Seville, (published by Editorial Starbooks, ed. Félix Escrig and José Sanche), 18–20 September 2013.

Lecture Notes

Schenk, Mark, 'Origami in Engineering and Architecture: An Art Spanning Mathematics, Engineering and Architecture', 2012. Published online: http://www.markschenk.com/research/teaching/ArchEng2012_lecture_web.pdf [accessed 14.01.15].

Pérez Valcárcel, Juan, 'Movilidad de Grandes Estructuras', ETSA Universidade da Coruña. Published online: http://www.perezpinero.org/PDF/VALCARCEL_Movilidad_grandes_estructuras.pdf [accessed 14.01.15].

Letter

From Kenneth Snelson to R Motro. *International Journal of Space Structures, Tensegrity*. University of Surrey, Guildford, 1990. Published online: http://www.grunch.net/snelson/rmoto.html [accessed 14.01.15].

Essay

Heartney, Eleanor, 'Forces Made Visible', in *Kenneth Snelson, Art and Ideas*. Published online: http://kennethsnelson.net/KennethSnelson_Art_And_Ideas.pdf [accessed 14.01.15].

Interview

Interview with Dr Zhong You by Esther Rivas Adrover, 21 December 2006.

Exhibition Containing Early Kinetic /Deployable Art

Royal Academy of Arts. *RADICAL GEOMETRY 1930s, Modern Art of South America from the Patricia Phelps de Cisneros Collection*. Curated by Adrian Locke. London. 2014.

INDEX

INDEX

PICTURE CREDITS
& ACKNOWLEDGEMENTS

**All images © Esther Rivas Adrover,
except the following:**

pp23–24 figs 1–3: Britt, Alan L. and Lalvani, Haresh.
IUTAM-IASS Symposium. **pp25–26 figs 4–11:** Maria
Lardi. Redrawn from Britt, Alan L. and Lalvani, Haresh.
IUTAM-IASS Symposium. **p27 fig 1; p28 fig 2;**
p29 fig 4: Milo Ayden De Luca. Redrawn from Yan Chen
and Zhong You United States Patent Number: 6,941,704
B2. 2005. **pp30–33:** Pete Silver. **p35 fig 1:** Eirini Krasaki.
p35 fig 2: Eirini Krasaki. Redrawn from Chuck Hoberman.
p38 fig 2; p39 fig 3: Milo Ayden De Luca. Redrawn
from Charles Hoberman United States Patent Number:
5,024,031. 1991. **p42 fig1; p43 fig 2:** Eirini Krasaki.
Redrawn from Tomomi Kanemitsu, Shinji Matsumoto,
Haruyuki Namba, Takanori Sato, Hisato Tadokoro,
Takao Oura, Kenji Takagi, Shigeru Aoki and Nobuyuki
Kaya, IUTAM-IASS Symposium. **p45 figs 3–5; pp46–47
figs 6–8:** Frank Vadstrup Jensen and Sergio Pellegrino.
p48 fig 1; p49 figs 2–3; p51 figs 7–9: Frank Vadstrup
Jensen and Sergio Pellegrino. IASS Journal and IASS
Symposium. **p50 figs 4–6:** Will McLean. **pp52–3
figs 1–3:** Adam Kalkin. **p54 fig 1; p57 fig 5:** Studio
Gang Architects. **pp55–56 figs 2–3:** © Greg Murphy.
p56 fig 4: © Mike Graham. **pp60–61 figs 1–4:**
Birds Portchmouth Russum Architects. **p65 figs 1–2:**
Lindstrand Technologies. **p67 figs 1–3; p94 fig 1;**
p99 figs 1–3: Milo Ayden De Luca. Redrawn from Gunnar
Tibert. **p69 fig 1:** Milo Ayden De Luca. Redrawn from
Sergio Pellegrino. **p70 fig 2:** ATK Engineering Company,
Space Components Division, California. **pp70–73
figs 3–4:** © NASA. **pp76–77 figs 1–4:** © Fundación
Emilio Pérez Piñero. **p79 figs 1–2:** Félix Escrig,
Juan Pérez Valcárcel and José Sanchez. IASS Journal.
p80 figs 3–8: Félix Escrig, Juan Pérez Valcárcel and José
Sanchez. **p82 fig 2:** Milo Ayden De Luca. Redrawn
from K. Kawaguchi, IUTAM-IASS Symposium. **pp83–87
figs 1–4:** Mark Stepheson from Soundforms Ltd, Jason
Flanagan and Paul Bavister of Flanagan Lawrence, Ian
Knowles of Arup acoustic and ESGroup. **pp95 figs 2–4;
p96 fig1; p97 fig 2–5; p99 fig 4; pp100-101 figs
5–8:** Gunnar Tibert. **pp106–107 figs 1–3; pp108-109
figs 5–6:** Maciej Piekarski. IUTAM-IASS Symposium.
p107 fig 4: Marian Misiakiewicz. IUTAM-IASS Symposium.
pp110–113; figs 1–6; pp120–123 figs 1–5: Tomohiro
Tachi. **pp114–119:** Tomohiro Tachi, Motoi Masubuchi
and Masaaki Iwamoto. **pp124-125:** Weina Wu and
Zhong You. © Royal Society. **p129 fig 1; p130 fig 2;**

p131 fig 3: Milo Ayden De Luca. Redrawn from J. H.
Brackenbury, IUTAM-IASS Symposium. **p132 fig 1:**
B. Kresling. **p133 fig 2:** B. Kresling. © Royal Society.
p134 fig 3: H. Kobayashi, B. Kresling and J. F. V. Vincent.
© Royal Society. **p135 fig 1:** Plant Biomechanics Group
Freiburg & ITKE Universität Stuttgart. © IOP Publishing.
Reproduced with permission. All rights reserved.
p137 fig 2: ITKE / Julian Lienhard. © IOP Publishing.
Reproduced with permission. All rights reserved.
pp137–138 figs 3–4: ITKE / Julian Lienhard.
p139 fig 6: Iijima, T., Sibaoko, T. (1981). Action Potential
in the Trap-lobes of Aldrovanda vesiculosa. Plant & Cell
Physiol. 22 (8), 1595-1601. **p140 fig 5:** Howard Mao.
pp141–143 figs 7–11: ITKE / Simon Schleicher.
© IABSE-IASS Symposium London 2011.

Acknowledgements

Contributors' work has been credited throughout
the publication and the picture credits.

Special thanks to Milo Ayden De Luca, Maria Lardi and
Eirini Krasaki for their outstanding work on redrawing.
I would like to thank Julian Vincent, Gunnar Tibert and
Mark Schenk for not only providing their own work
but for pointing me towards other important sources
and information. I would like to thank Keith Seffen for
sparing time to show me the former DSL (Deployable
Structures Laboratory) in the University of Cambridge
and sharing his knowledge on the subject. I would also
like to extend my gratitude to Zhong You, who has
kindly made his deployable laboratory in the University
of Oxford available to me on several occasions and who
agreed to an interview. A million thanks to Pete Silver,
Leo Peter Silver and J. E. A. Silver.

This book was inspired by research produced by the
author in her postgraduate studies of Architecture in
2006 at Oxford Brookes University under the tutors
Matt Gaskin and Helena Webster. I would also like
to extend my appreciation to Igea Troiani for several
useful conversations. I am also grateful to John Assael,
of Assael Architecture, who kindly provided a
scholarship to support this investigation. I would
specially like to thank Nick J. McGough for his support
and inspiration.